RÖTTGER

Creative clay design

ERNST RÖTTGER

Creative Clay Design

NEW YORK **Reinhold Publishing Corporation**

Published in the United States of America 1963
by Reinhold Publishing Corporation
Library of Congress Catalog Card Number 63-8676
Printed in Holland

Reprinted 1964
Reprinted 1965
Reprinted 1967

FOREWORD

This is the third volume of a series of books which are the results of a decade's work. I have been asked to write the foreword. I can imagine nothing better than writing about a material which appeals so strongly and directly to our creative instincts.

Clay in particular has always had an almost magical attraction for children. They are drawn to it, they seize a lump of it and discover, as is shown in this book, that the shapeless lump is transformed into a cylinder, or perhaps a cone, and at once they perceive a whole new world of possibilities.

In my mind's eye I can imagine a child's first encounter with clay: no matter what the place or the time the scene will be the same whether it occurred in a cave of the Ice Age, in ancient Egypt or in a country village today. A group of children stands watching the eldest boy, perhaps five years of age, who is busy modelling. 'That's you and that's the dog and that is our goat', says the artist and quickly sticks two horns on to the goat to distinguish it from the dog. The little girl stares open-mouthed at this work of art and whispers, 'Is that me?' The young creator nods assent and watches proudly as she carefully bears the little figures away to safe-keeping.

Their mother, however, long inured against astonishment at her own children, has a spring-clean and throws the little lumps of clay out of the cave; she stops for a moment, turning over a few little bowls in her hand . . . If these could be made bigger we could . . . then we could at last keep everything in order. She looks into the future—larders, storerooms—for she has already begun to sow corn and has trouble in storing the different grains apart. This would be a way of keeping them separate.

Thus perhaps did the potter's craft originate: but the first impulse towards it was surely that of sheer pleasure in creation.

Hans Leistikow

CONTENTS

INTRODUCTION

Malleable materials such as mortar, clay, plasticine and wax make an immediate appeal to the sense of touch and to the will to create. Every person of normal sensibility, but above all a child, has by nature both the urge and the ability to give form to any shapeless mass. The first shapes which the child makes from any pliable material are seldom valid forms in themselves. They acquire their meaning from the child who perceives in them, as in his first attempts at drawing, a multitude of shapes according to his fancy.

However, when this stage of free play comes to an end, and with the city-bred child it is usually terminated all too soon, some guidance is then required in order to counteract the mass of negative influences which begin to affect him. Many parents and teachers make mistakes in this critical stage of the child's development whose effect is to reduce enjoyment in creative activity and to stunt the growth of originality and inventiveness. In my experience, it is a fundamental error to give a child too small quantities of material for modelling. It is often said that the clay is too expensive. Some people also tend to believe that their 'dear little ones' should make 'nice little things'. This viewpoint leads to modelling with the fingers only instead of the whole hand and to overvaluation of small single pieces. Experience, however, confirms again and again that children like to work on a large scale, in drawing and painting as much as in plastic modelling. One only has to watch children playing with sand or observe their absorption in building a snowman to see this. As much as by insufficient quantities of material both children and adult beginners are hindered in their development by using ready-made figure moulds.

Only a few modest tools are needed to supplement the hands:

1 Piece of wire and a kitchen knife for cutting.

2 Short length of wood for beating.

3 Rolling pin.

4 Sponge for smoothing-off.

5 Home-made punch for impressing pattern.

The material to be used is potter's clay, which is preferable to all others for its qualities:

1 It is a natural substance dug straight from the ground.
2 Being cheap it can be obtained in large quantities.
3 It can be modelled in a damp state, cut in a leather-hard state and in the dry state buffed, polished, fired, painted and glazed.
4 When unfired it can always be reduced to a plastic state and used again.

This book purposely mentions only the minimum of technical instructions. It gives examples which are intended to guide the layman and teacher in systematic sequence towards an awakening of the creative imagination. Therefore the pieces illustrated, the results of teaching based on years of experience, are not to be regarded as examples for copying. They are meant only to demonstrate the variety which can be achieved by these methods with children, adult pupils and students. Even the most modest of these examples are, from an educational point of view, more valuable than the most perfect imitations. The object is to awaken the elemental joy in creative work and to avoid the disappointment which can result from unplanned handling of plastic materials.

Kassel, March 1962

Ernst Röttger

CHARACTERISTICS

The basis of all creative activity is order. Pictorial creation consists in an ordering of shapes and colours which is strongly conditioned by the particular nature of the plastic medium.

Clay is a medium whose great pliability can easily lead to disorderly and slap-dash modelling. Therefore in clay modelling the working process should be more closely supervised than in the use of other materials.

As in all true play-forms, the results of playing with plastic material are never known. The meaning of the game does not lie in the functional use of what is produced but in the play itself, in a liberating activity which is particularly healthy and satisfying for people in this mechanised age. Anybody who in play succeeds in learning the characteristics of the material and in gaining creative experience will then be able to give significant form to functional objects, as many examples in this book will show.

SYMBOLS

S = Work produced by students of the State High School of Applied Arts, Kassel.

A = Work by amateurs, mostly from adult education classes

B = Work by boys

G = Work by girls

The small figures indicate the age of the executant.

ACKNOWLEDGMENT

Examples of their pupils' work for illustration in this volume were supplied by the following:

Hans Dobe: Figures 84, 88, 102-4, 108, 111, 128, 162, 172, 173, 184, 240, 241 and 243

Heinz Hüttel: Figure 214

Photographs and photographic work by Dieter Klante, with the exception of the following illustrations which were taken by:

Hermann Michel, Munich: Figures 123, 124, 132-4, 163 and 164

Friedhelm Tschentscher, Kassel: Figures 195 and 196

1

2

FIRST EXERCISES

Shaping the Ball of Clay

BASIC SHAPES

The shapeless mass of the prepared and slightly damp clay is divided into lumps as large as clenched fists. The clay should not be too damp. To change a rough clay ball into a simple geometrical body with flat, rounded, concave or convex sides, the clay should be worked without the use of any tools. The lumps should only be beaten, rolled and kneaded on the tabletop.

Nothing should be added to or removed from the clay body. These and the following exercises are—apart from their formal position in the series—excellently suited to the purpose of learning the properties of clay. The behaviour of the clay body when it is struck, beaten, rolled, kneaded, thrown, split or twisted demonstrates its plasticity and the degree to which this depends on consistency and moisture content. Complete familiarity with the material is the essential precondition of knowing how to exploit its plastic qualities.

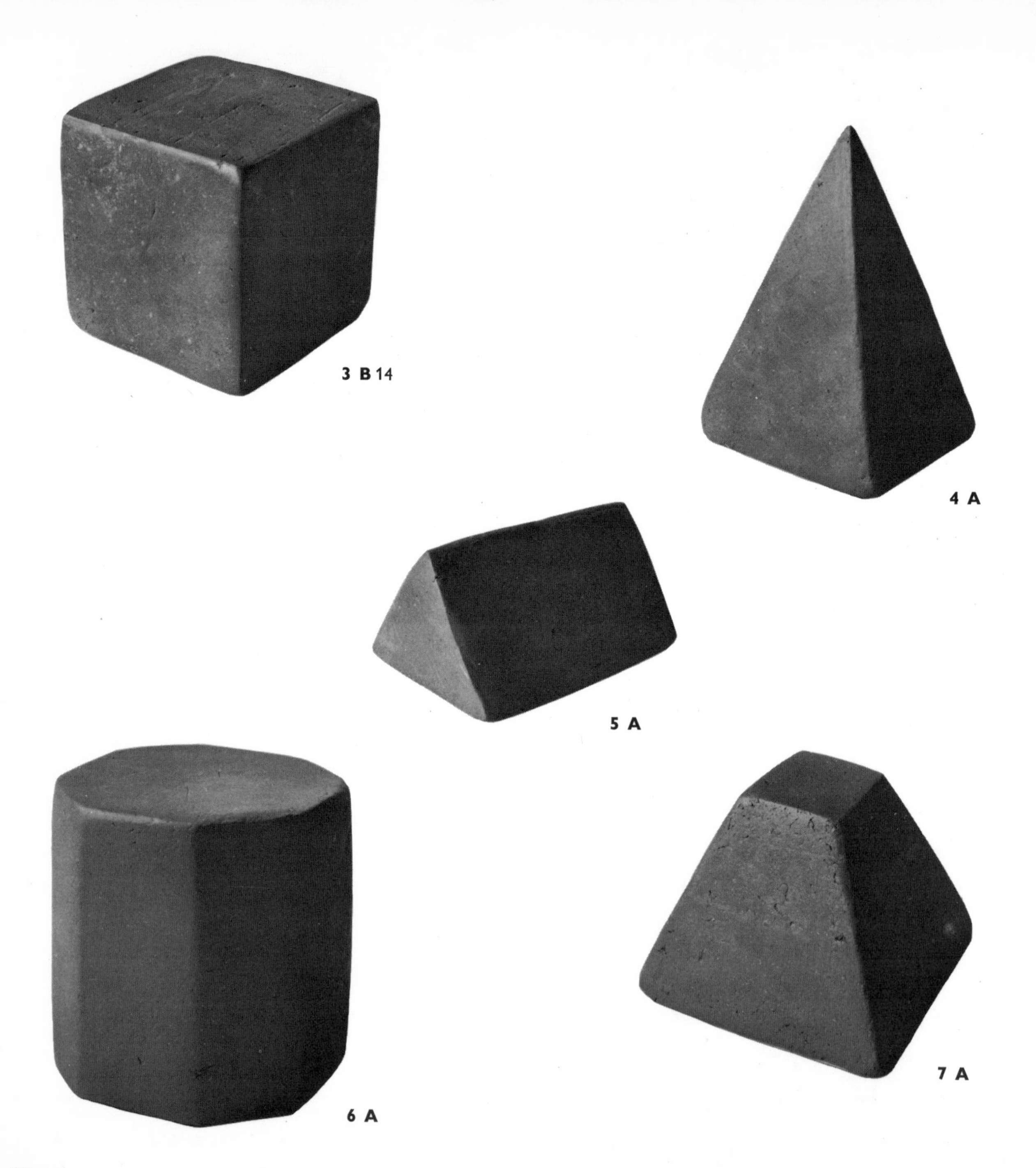
3 B 14
4 A
5 A
7 A
6 A

Figures 3-11: shapes produced by beating, rolling and kneading the lump of clay.

It is advisable to begin with simple shapes such as spheres, blocks and cubes. It is not as easy as it may seem to give the required shape to the formless material.

A certain degree of experience in handling the material is required to be able to make pyramids, truncated pyramids, prisms and cubes. First the rough shape is produced by banging the lump on the table and it is then fashioned by careful beating.

12 B 14

13 A

DEVELOPMENT OF BASIC SHAPES

A wooden ruler is the only tool required for the following exercises.

First steps consist in simple basic shapes made by beating the clay on the tabletop. They are then given further shape by being patted with the ruler.

Figures 12, 13: cube and cylinder shapes developed by smacking the corners or edges with a ruler.

Figures 14-18: five different results of the same exercise. A bar is altered by gentle knocking until it evolves into a new shape, although the original form should still be recognisable.

There is a striking affinity between this clay work and pieces of wrought iron. Red-hot wrought iron has in fact a plasticity very similar to that of partially dried clay. This is most clearly shown in Figures 20-25.

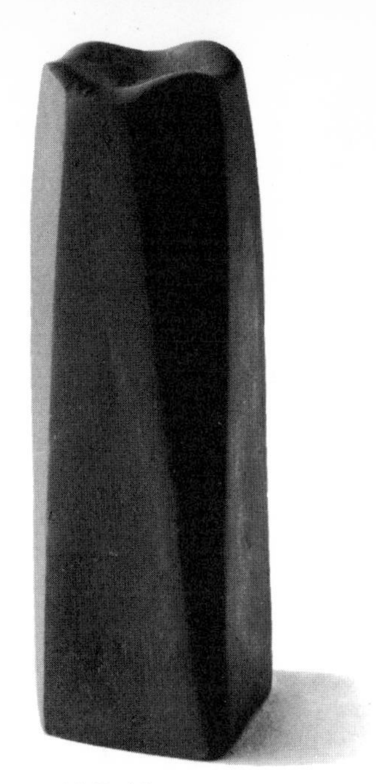

14 B 14

15 B 14

16 B 13

17 B 14

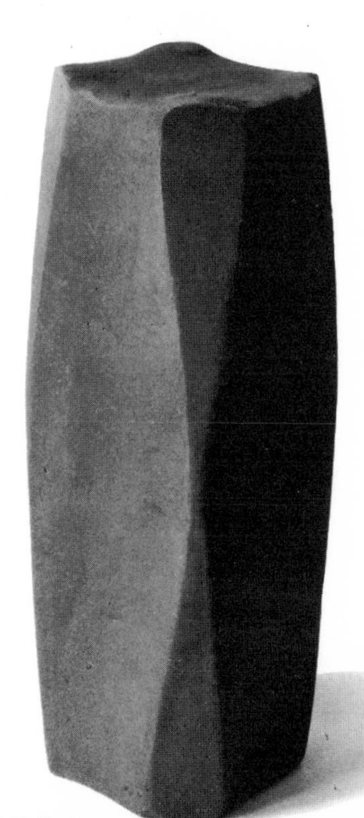

18 B 15

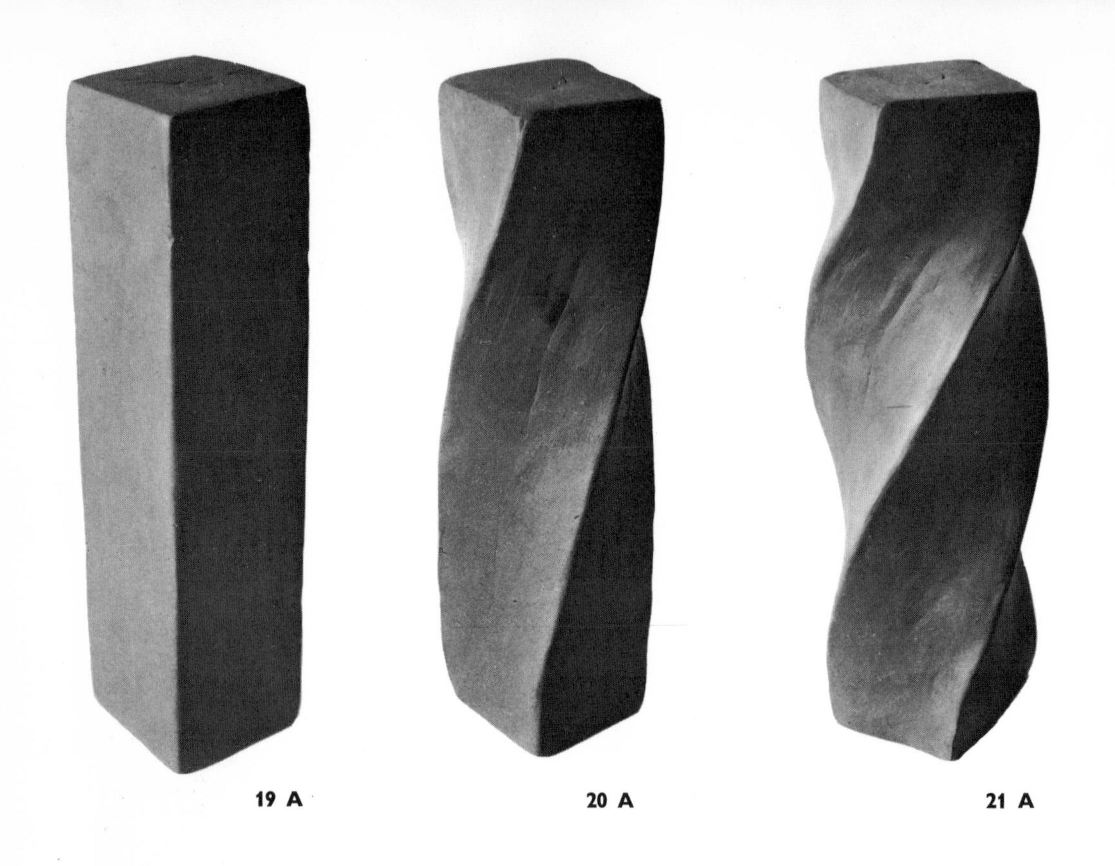

19 A 20 A 21 A

A few ways in which the basic shape can be altered by twisting, splitting and bending. A knife is used to split the clay. Here it is essential for the clay to have exactly the correct moisture content; it sags if it is too damp and snaps if too dry.

Figures 19-21: how a bar can be twisted. The full extent is reached in Figure 21.

Figures 22-25: how a bar can be bent and split. Figure 24 shows how far this treatment can be taken.

22 A

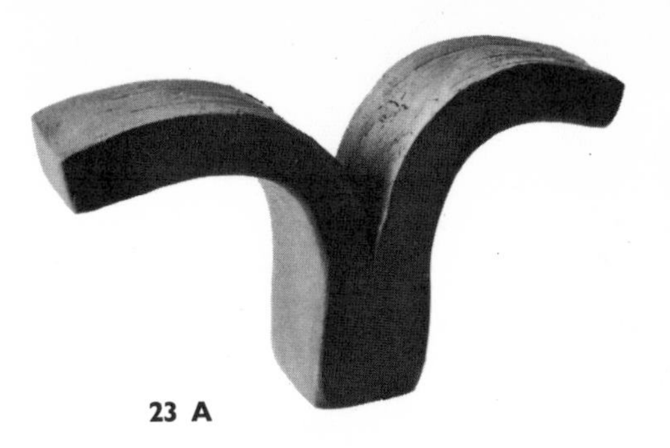

23 A

24 A

25 A

26 S

27 S

28 S

29 S

30 B 14

31 B 14

32 S

Simple shapes are divided and rearranged to create new, articulated shapes.

No clay should be added or taken away.

Tools: a knife or cutting wire.

Figures 26-28, 30: new shapes developed by splitting up the basic form and repositioning the parts.

Figure 29: divided organic shape whose halves are slightly offset.

Figures 31, 32: geometric bodies whose component sections are reversed or (figure 32) placed in another sequence and partially reversed.

33

34 A

A well-proportioned plastic structure is built up from a basic cubic shape by cutting out smaller cubes and repositioning them.

No material should be added or taken away.

Figure 33 illustrates the method.

These exercises, on the building-block principle, have a marked play character. When the cube is dissected and the pieces reassembled to make a different shape, the possible combinations are so numerous that it is advisable to limit the scope of this exercise by clearly defined rules, e.g. to specify the shape, size and number of the pieces to be cut out and the way in which they are to be applied (upwards, lengthways, sideways, etc.). When pupils have gained some experience in this exercise they can be given greater freedom in execution.

35 A

36 A

37 A

38 A

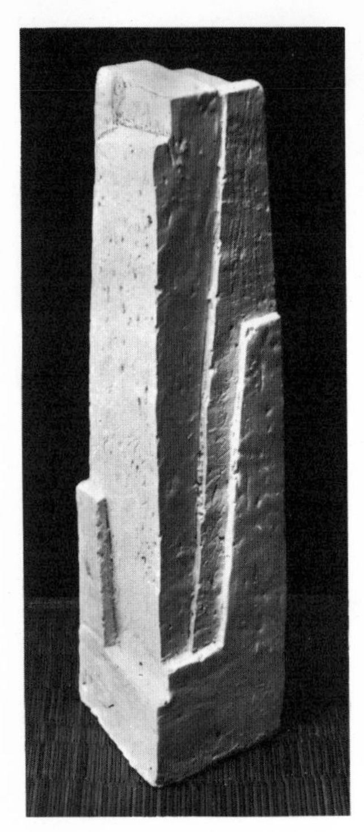

39 S

40 S

41 S

42 S

In all previous exercises a basic form is reshaped without taking away any of the material. Here a body is given shape and proportion by cutting away part of its substance.

Exercise: lines and planes are cut into the surface of a simple geometric body in such a way as to produce an original, articulated plastic shape.

No more should be cut away than allows the original shape to remain recognisable. The rules should lay down the method of achieving the required effect (direction or number of cuts, depth of gradations, type of structure, etc.).

Figures 39-42: carved from plaster of Paris, which for these exercises is equally as suitable as leather-hard clay.

Figures 43, 45: these examples show how much greater are the expressive qualities of ceramic material. The surfaces have been partially roughened to show the effectiveness of contrasts in texture.

43 A

44 S

45 S

46 S

47 S

48 A

49 A

Figures 48, 49: a good solution to the problem of turning a bar of clay into the shape of a fish. It will be clearly seen how the rule of removing as little material as possible from the basic shape has been strictly observed.

50 A

51 A

52 B 14

Exercise: a cubic shape is pierced from the sides and hollowed out into a complex of spatial rectangles. The resulting internal spaces should bear a sound rhythmic relationship to one another and to the basic shape; the outer edges of the basic shape should remain unaltered. Precise instructions determine the way in which the exercise is carried out; in this case the clay is best cut when in the leather-hard state. A knife is the only tool required. Finishing touches can be added to the various elements of the structure when the material has dried out. The grained effect of the structure in Figure 55 is achieved by scraping with a knife. Not only cubes but other forms (bar, sphere, cone) can be articulated by cutting out.

53 B 14

54 B 14

55 S

56 B 10

57 **B** 10

Plaster of Paris is introduced into this book only as a supplementary medium to the sculpturally more satisfactory medium of clay. The use of plaster in liquid form, its use as a modelling material in stucco-work and the making of plaster casting moulds are all processes of such complexity that to describe them would fill a whole book. The following section will be limited to relief in slabs and blocks.

RELIEF

A knife or punch is used to cut out shapes from a slab of plaster at varying levels so as to produce a design in relief. Cutting can either be started without a plan and the design created by extension while working, or a drawing is prepared beforehand and then transferred to the slab. Before cutting, the plaster should be slightly moistened. The material will cut more easily and irritation from dust is reduced.

THE MASK

The mask has always been a favourite object of plastic design. Its expressive potential has long served religion and drama and still has a function in our own times. Children bring to making masks the same enjoyment with which they change their features by wearing them.

Figures 56 and 57 show masks cut by children from blocks of plaster which in their expressive intensity recall mediaeval architectural ornaments. The difference in results produced by the various methods of working can be seen by comparing the examples on Pages 34, 48 and 57.

Shapes from Clay Slabs

The clay slab offers an almost unlimited variety of potential exercises in creative activity. The following pages show exercises ranging from the simple treatment of planes through relief and spatial forms to designs of architectural character. The attempt is also made to indicate a clear and methodical sequence of development and thereby to point the way to new and increasingly satisfying forms of treatment; the examples given here are by no means exhaustive. With these exercises, too, much of their worth lies in their purely formal aspect of training in artistic discipline, i.e. activating and channelling the creative powers latent in every person. Therefore their functional value must be regarded as secondary, although 'practical' values are by no means lacking in them and the experience gained in executing them is essentially applicable to the design of genuinely functional articles.

The preparation of a clay slab is simplicity itself. A slab can either be sliced from a well kneaded and shaped block or a lump of clay can be flattened into a slab with a rolling pin and then cut to the required shape.

SURFACE TEXTURE BY FINGER IMPRINT

The first tools are simply the fingers. The exercise consists of texturing the surface of the slab by finger pressure, starting with free experimentation in order to acquire the 'feel' of the material and its plasticity. After this initial stage of 'play' the creative process should be formalised and guided by certain rules. Page 29 shows the results of exercises of this type, using either simple finger pressure or the index finger and thumb grip. The exercise series is: sequences of similar forms, sequences in opposite direction (movement and counter-movements), texturing by patterns of equal or varying sizes, etc.

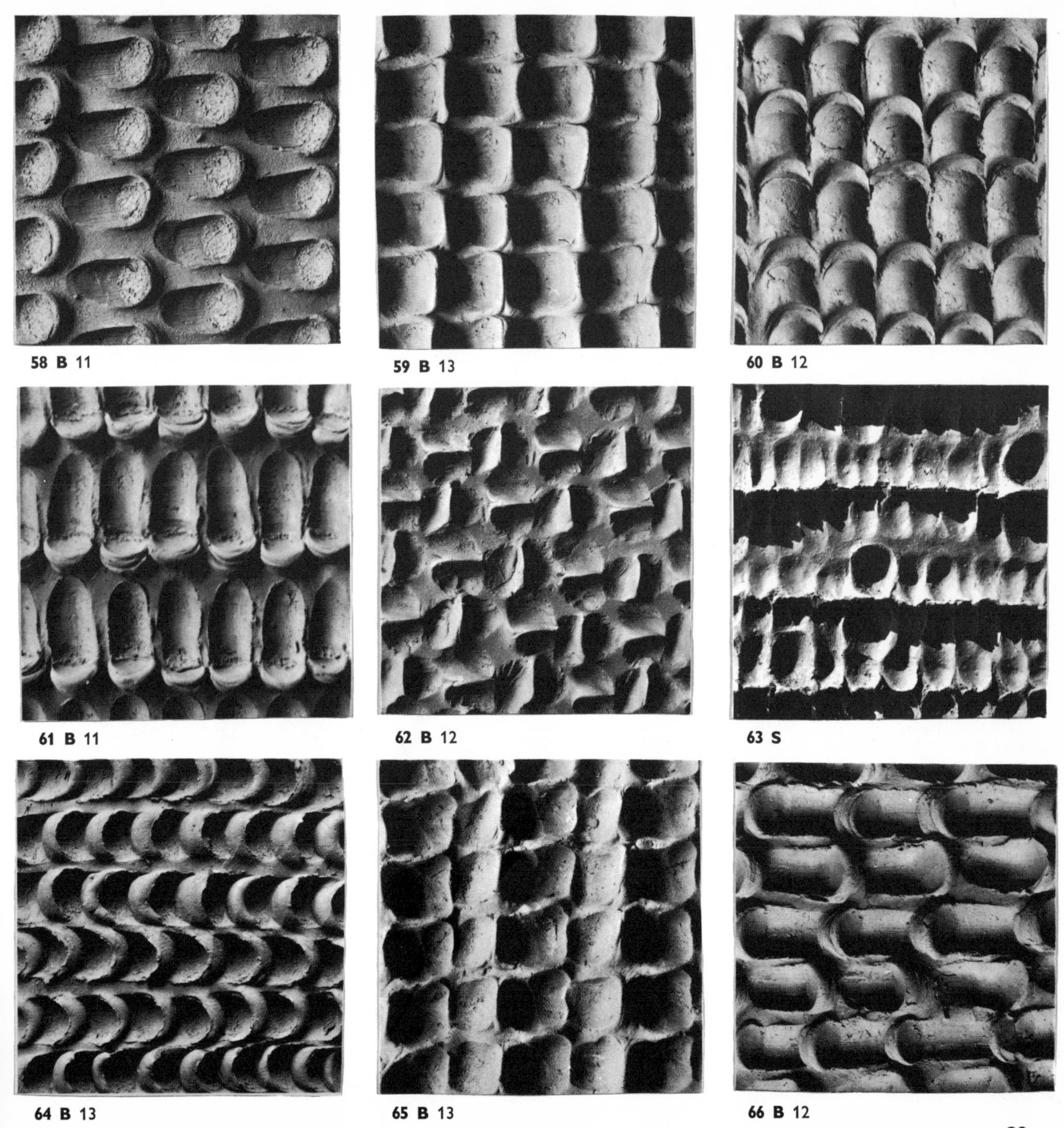

58 B 11

59 B 13

60 B 12

61 B 11

62 B 12

63 S

64 B 13

65 B 13

66 B 12

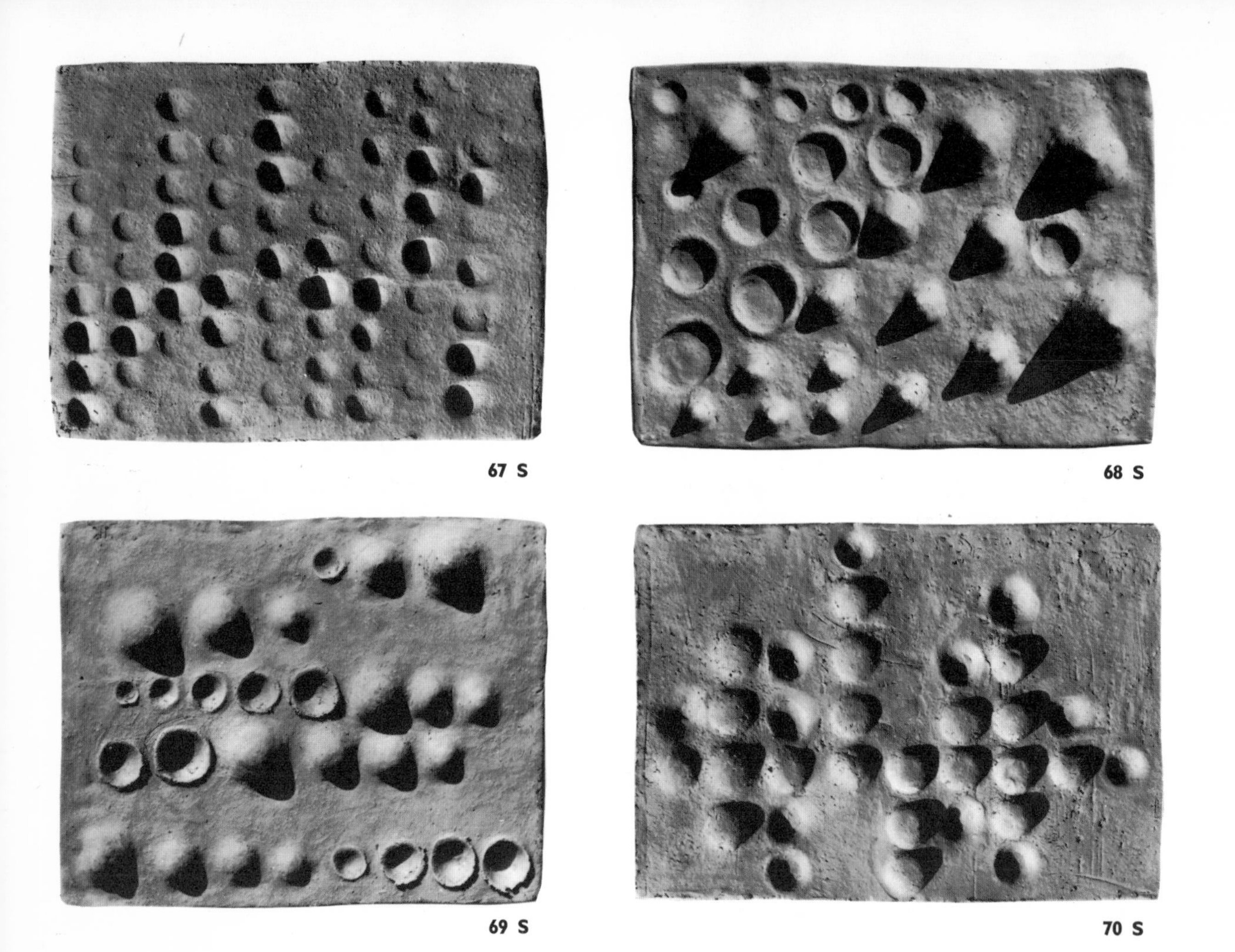

67 S

68 S

69 S

70 S

For texturing exercises the clay must be kept somewhat damper than usual to allow patterning with light finger pressure. Wet clay adheres easily, so that when the slab is being rolled out it must be constantly turned over to stop it from sticking to the tabletop and tearing when it is pulled away.

Four examples of the transition from regular to random patterning. The plastic values of these slabs are created by the alternation of large and small, positive and negative relief patterns.

LINEAR TEXTURING

The following exercises also require only fingers as tools. Ridges are pressed out of the flattened slab with thumb and index finger. According to the type of grip either low (Figure 73) or sharp (Figure 74) ridges are produced.

The examples suggest a methodical sequence from simple linear texturing to figurative relief modelling. Relief slabs are particularly suited to grouping in large areas to form a textured composition (Figure 75).

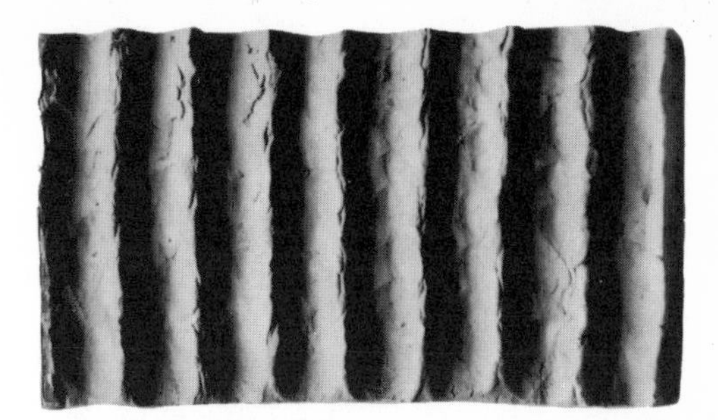

71 B 12

72 B 12

73 B 12

74 B 12

75 B 12

p. 48

I

76 B 12

77 B 13

78 B 12

79 B 13

Figurative reliefs squeezed out of the slab and partially textured by finger pressure (illustrations greatly reduced in size). In Figures 78 and 79 the outline of the natural object is used as the basic form before modelling.

80 G 11

81 B 14

82 B 13

83 B 14

84 B 13

85 G 15

86 G 15

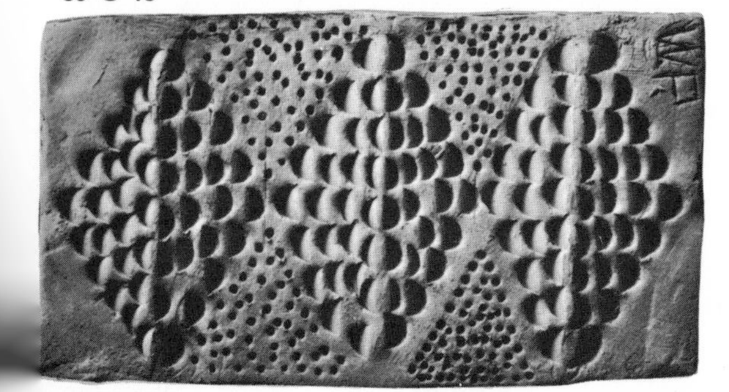

87 G 15

88 B 16

SURFACE TEXTURE BY STAMPING

This exercise begins with quite simple stamps. A strip of cardboard or piece of wood is sufficient at first; in fact the simpler the stamp the richer are the possible variations of design. All examples shown here were produced, with the exception of Figures 86 and 87, with pieces of cardboard or small pieces of wood. Having experimented with the possibilities of simple stamps such as these, other objects can be used such as nails, screws or keys. There are no limits to what the imagination may create with these means; it is only important that experimentation should not be uncontrolled but that while allowing full imaginative freedom the principles of order should be observed.

The final stage consists of cutting relief designs from wood or plaster (see Page 81).

89 S

Figure 89: design produced by pushing a piece of cardboard across soft clay.

Figures 90-92: three different results of the same exercise by schoolboys of the same age. Only two simple stamps should be used.

90 B 14

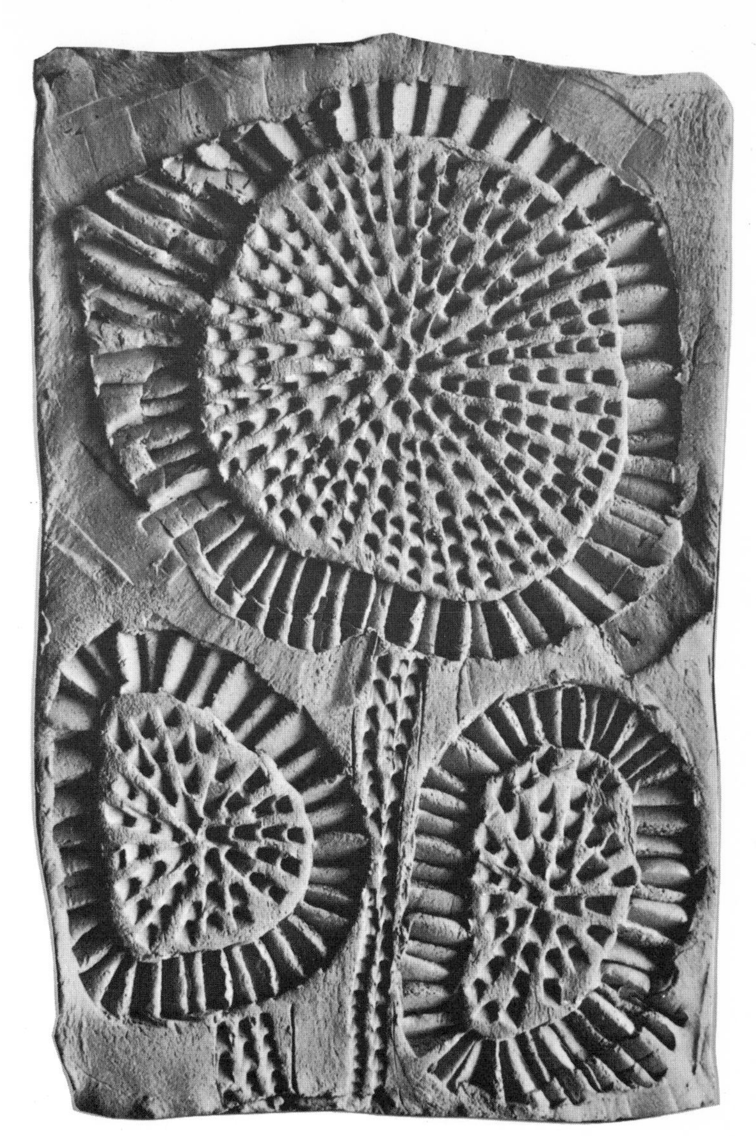

91 B 14

92 G 14

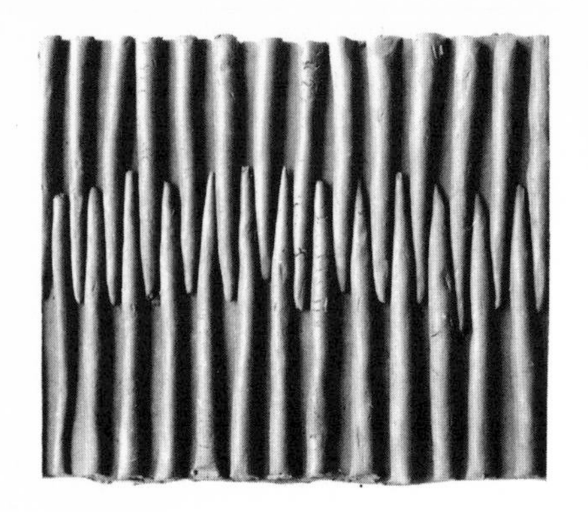

93 B 12

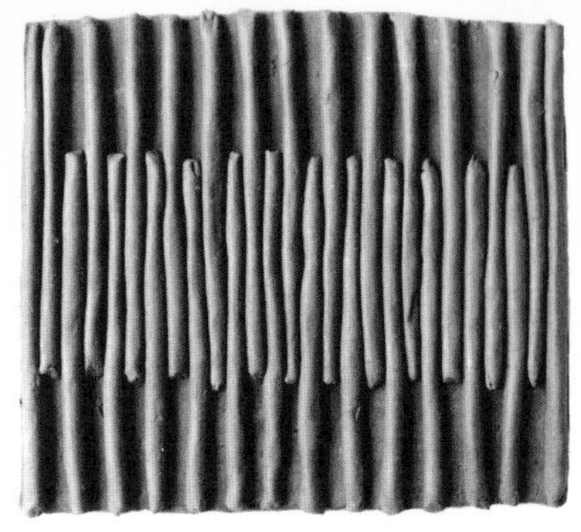

94 B 12

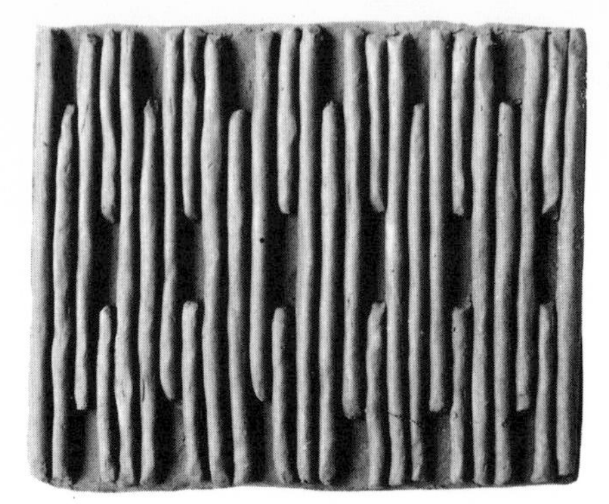

95 B 12

APPLIED SURFACE ORNAMENTATION

A lump of clay is rolled out on the tabletop into a roll of even thickness. A linear relief is produced by laying strips of the roll on to the damp clay slab. To allow the strips to adhere better it is advisable to dampen the clay slab slightly before application. The strips can either be kept round, in which case they must be very carefully applied in order to retain their shape, or they can be pressed firmly into the slab to produce flat-topped relief lines somewhat similar in effect to the lines squeezed out of the slab with finger and thumb.

Figures 93-99: various examples of vertical strip-ornamenting.

Figure 102: applied ornamentation with scales.

Figures 103, 104: figurative reliefs in which the strips are squeezed on to the slab.

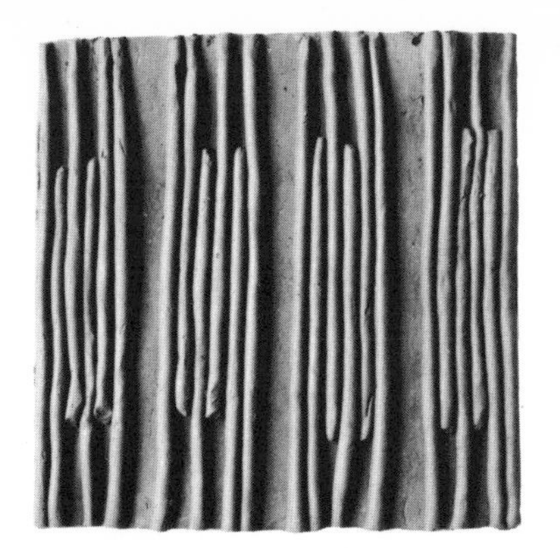

96 **B** 12

97 **B** 12

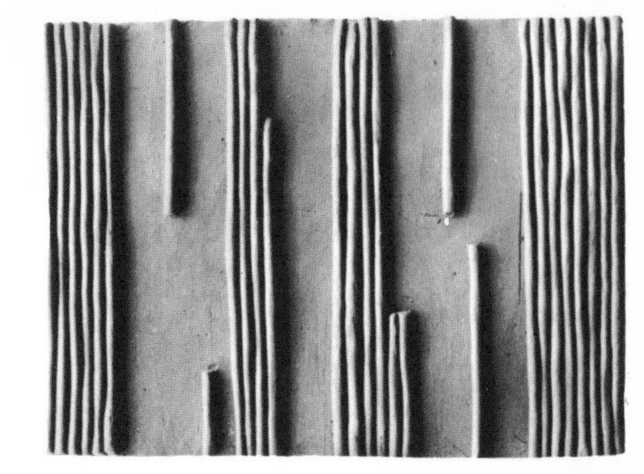

98 **B** 14

99 **B** 14

100 **B** 13

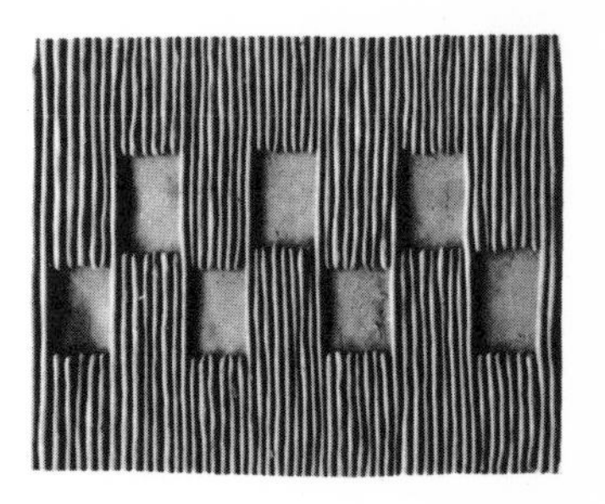

101 **B** 14

102 **B** 16

103 **B** 13

104 **B** 13

105 B 12

106 B 12

107 B 12

Figures 105-107: a methodical sequence showing how valid designs can be achieved by supplementing the outline with simple ornament.

Figures 109, 110: freer designs. The strips are partly squeezed on to the slab, partly directly applied, which produces a lively effect of contrast. Texture produced by small balls of clay.

Figure 112: a relief design composed of 25 slabs. Fired. Height 3 ft. 8 in., width 2 ft. The colour pattern is produced by using several types of clay.

108 B 12

109 B 12

110 B 12

111 B 12

112 S

113 B 14

114 B 14

115 S

SPATIAL FORMS FROM CLAY SLABS

In a soft state the clay slab can be bent in various directions to produce a spatial form. After the basic shape of the slab, the most important factors determining the forms are the characteristics of the clay itself, i.e. the composition of the body and moisture content.

These exercises are especially valuable for learning the mechanical properties of clay. The series begins quite simply. First of all upright rectangular slabs are bent to conform to simple linear patterns (angle, semi-circle, S-bend). In subsequent exercises the upright or horizontal slab is bent or rolled, sharply or gently, in various directions. Having begun with a rectangular slab, simple geometric forms (circle, semi-circle, triangle) or organic forms can be used as the basic shape. Later the slabs can be pierced or split or spatial forms can be constructed from several basic pieces.

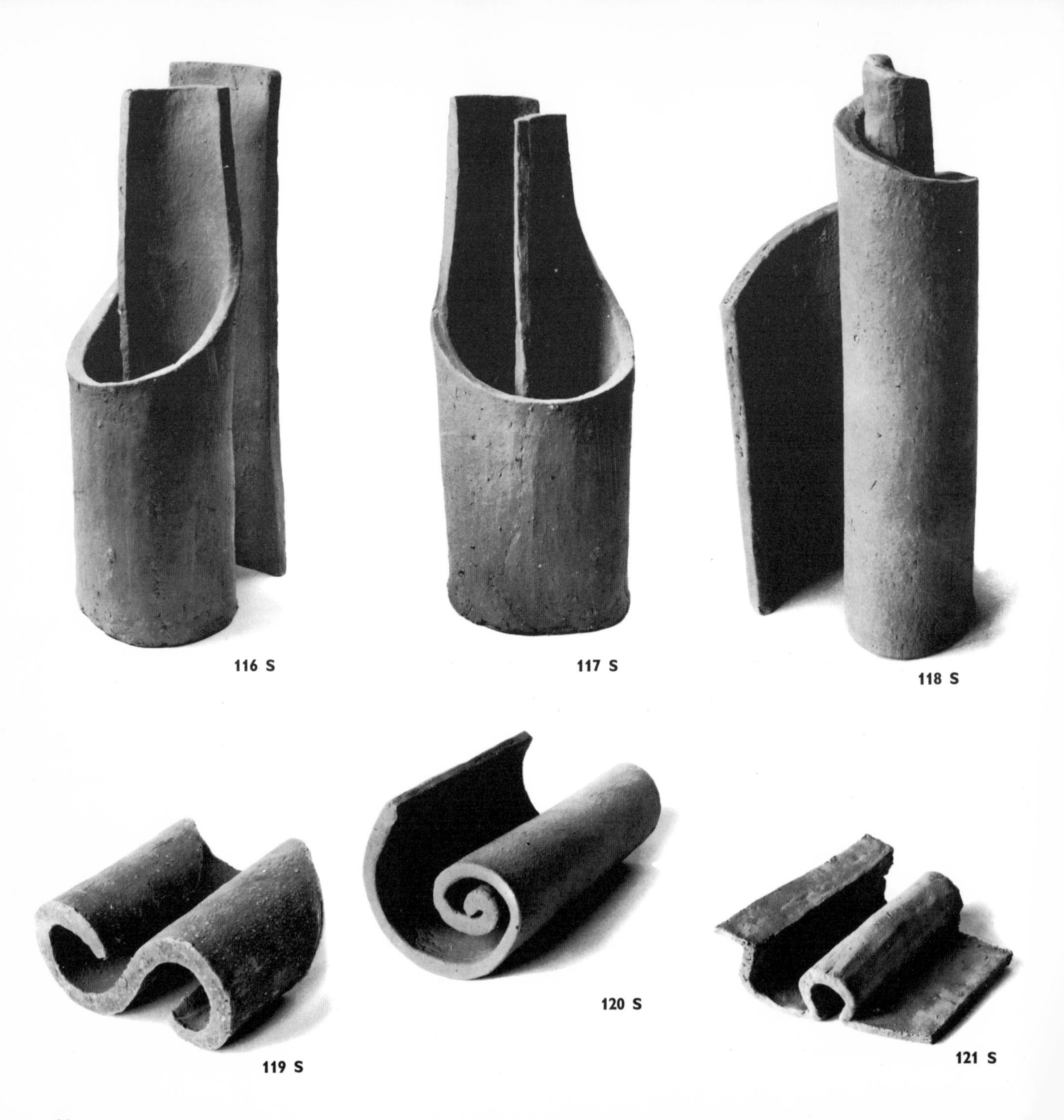

116 S

117 S

118 S

119 S

120 S

121 S

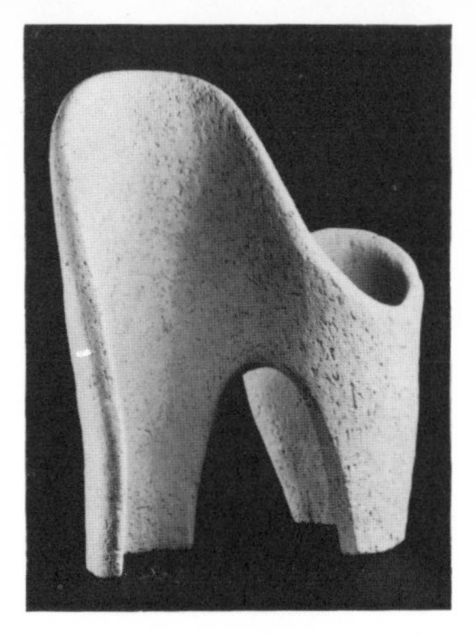

122 S

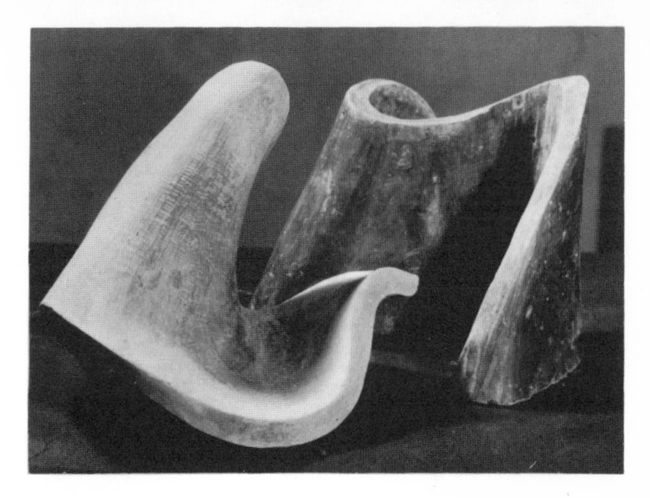

123 A

124 A

125 S

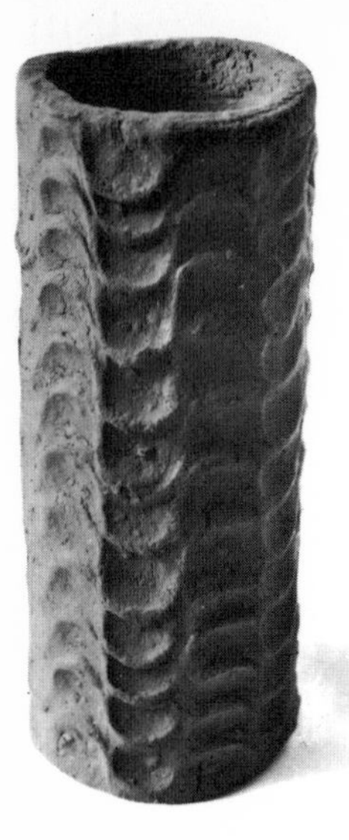

126 A

127 A

128 B 16

The shape shown in Figure 124 is especially remarkable among those illustrated on Page 45 for its strongly monumental effect. It demonstrates clearly how a simple, geometrically shaped basic piece can produce a strongly convincing effect even on a large scale. Imagine this piece, about 12 feet high, standing in the open.

Figures 126-128: a slab can be bent far enough to form a hollow shape. The examples chosen here are of slabs bent into tubes and textured by finger pressure and stamping. The seam is smoothed out. (This is the simplest method of forming a hollow vessel.)

Figure 129: slab articulated by cutting and bending out rectangular shapes.

Figure 130: rectangular cuts of varying sizes were made in the slab from opposite sides. The resulting strips were then rolled into the centre.

Figure 131: shape freely constructed from a simple slab.

129 S

130 S

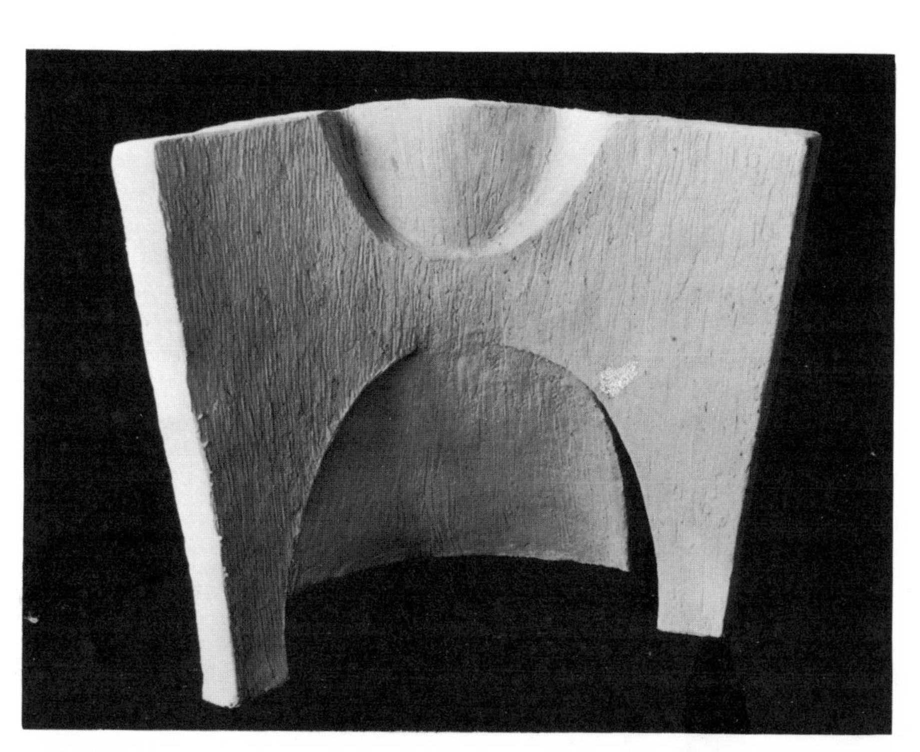

131 S

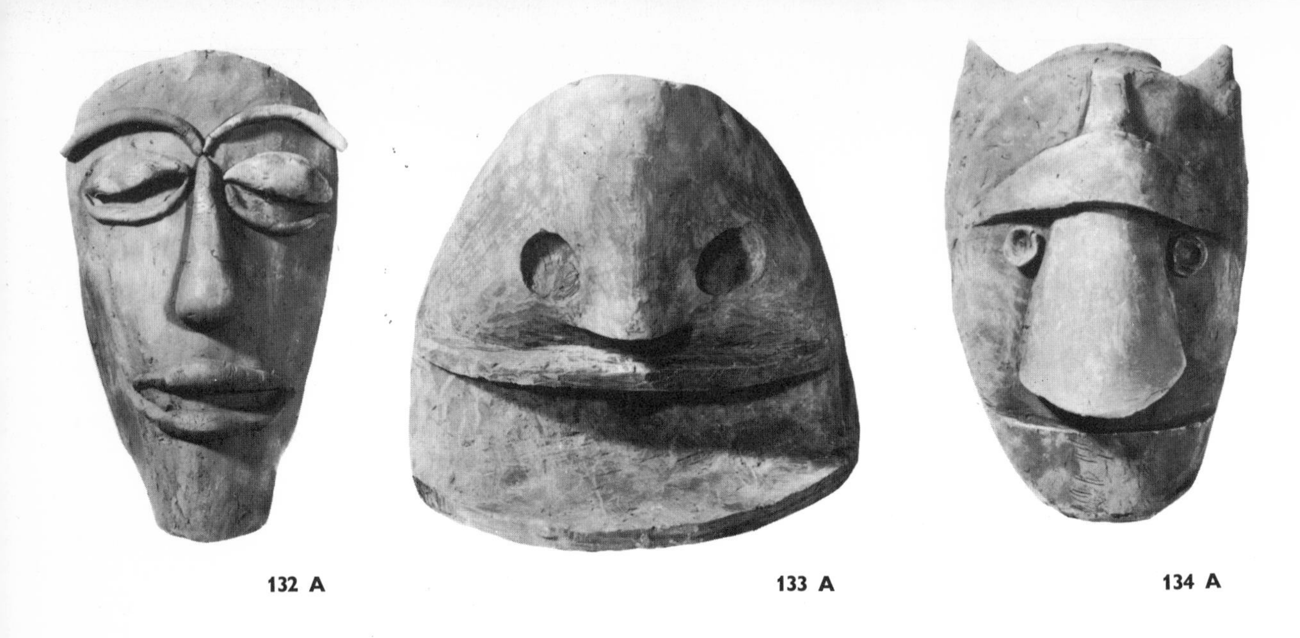

132 A

133 A

134 A

Figure 132: the basic shape consists of a bent slab; separately modelled detailing is then applied.

Figure 133: a curved slab; features are then cut into or pressed out of the basic form.

Figure 134: features built up from sections of slabs cut to shape.

Plate I (facing Page 32): mask shaped from a slab. The holes are cut when the clay is leather-hard. Fired. Slip coloured.

Plate II (opposite): spatial form built up from hollow boxes. When dry the surface is scratched with a knife to give texture, emphasising the very coarse grain of the body. Biscuit fired.

'Slip' and 'Biscuit' are explained on Page 94.

135 S

136 S

137 S

138 S

BOX MONTAGE

First, individual boxes are made up from clay slabs. The large plastic constructions are then assembled in a free arrangement of individual elements. The instructor should control the exercise by laying down, for instance, the shape, number and size of the boxes and indicating the direction of the build-up. Figure 136 shows a particularly effective rhythmic articulation in every dimension whereas the same construction seen from the other side does not achieve the same expressive power in the arrangement of spatial form.

Figures 138, 139: particularly effective spatial articulation, due to contrasts in size and position of the basic units. Functional objects, e.g. flower pots, can easily be developed from the shapes created in these exercises.

139 S

140 S

141 S

142 B 13

143 B 14

As with boxes, spatial constructions can also be built up with tubes formed from clay slabs. Here too it is advisable to begin with tubes of equal dimension or length and only gradually to introduce different sizes. The tubes can also be incised or pierced and experiments could be made with constructions of conical or barrel-shaped tubes.

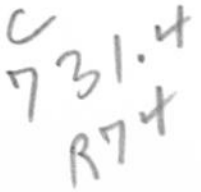

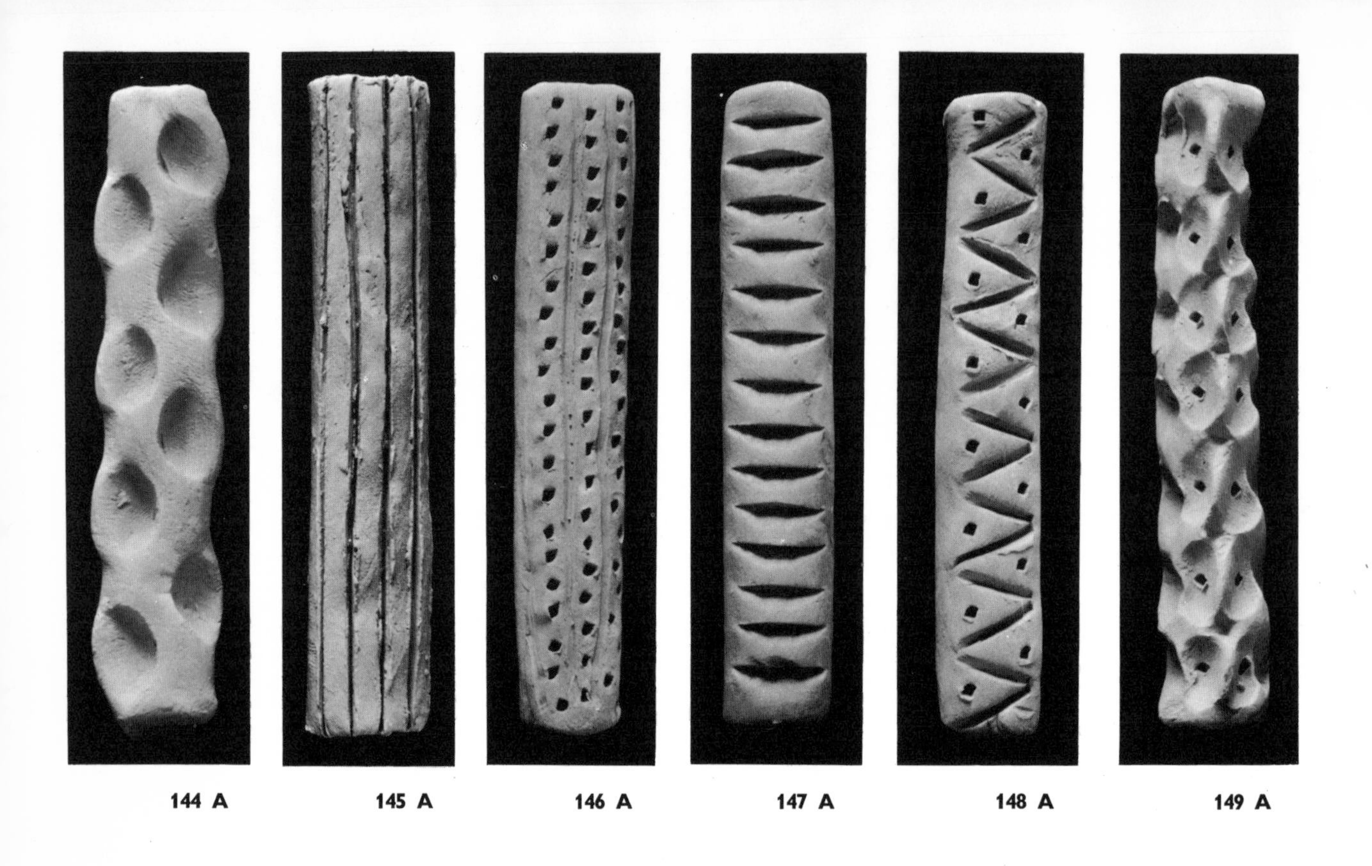

144 A 145 A 146 A 147 A 148 A 149 A

Shapes from Strips and Rolls of Clay

The basic shapes for the next exercises consist of strips cut from a clay slab and bars, formed by rolling out the strips.

Figures 144-149: examples of shapes from bars made by texturing with fingers, stamp, knife or nails.

150 S

151 S

Exercise: To build up regular or irregular compositions from rhythmically alternating strips and bars. Plastic expressivity may be heightened by applied or excised sections (Figures 150, 151).

152

Building up Hollow Pieces

VESSELS

The simplest and probably the oldest method of making hollow clay vessels is by building them up with rolls of clay. Roll a lump of clay into a ball on the tabletop, then elongate it and continue until it forms a long roll of uniform diameter; the thickness of the roll will depend on the size of vessel to be made. First make the base. A roll is twisted into a spiral disc of the required size and the disc is then smoothed out on both sides with the fingers. The build-up can now be undertaken in either of two ways:

1 The roll is laid round the edge of the disc and wound upwards in a spiral, a new roll simply being added as each one is finished.

2 Single rolls are added on as rings. Care should be taken to vary the position of the joints of successive rings.

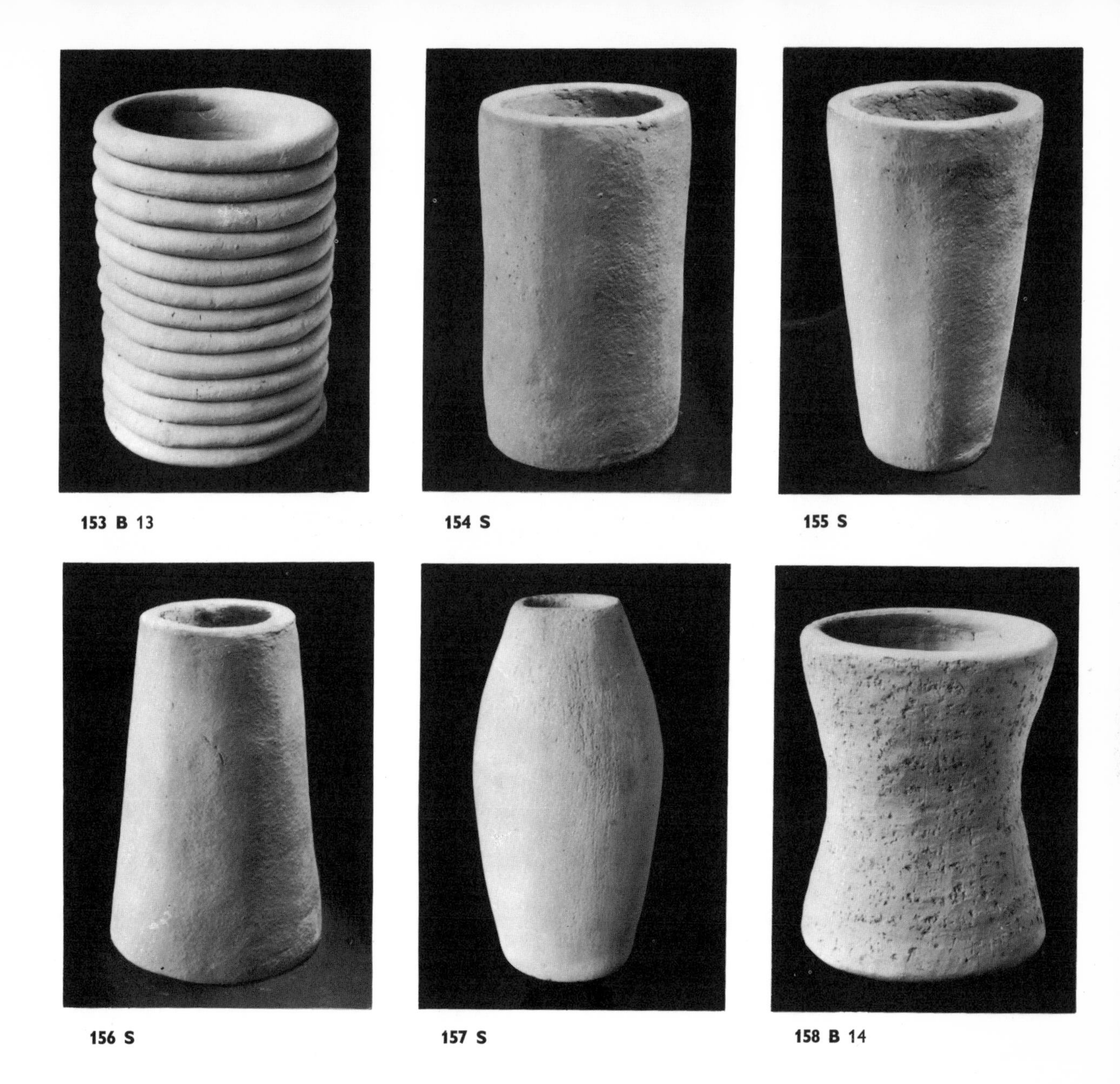

153 B 13

154 S

155 S

156 S

157 S

158 B 14

159 S

160 S

161 S

As with the base, so the rings forming the wall must be smoothed off on both sides. This makes the wall thinner. If a thicker wall is required, a thin extra roll should be laid in each groove before they are smoothed down. It is advisable to cover the prepared rolls with a damp cloth, otherwise they tend to dry out quickly and become brittle. The shape of the vase depends on the way the wall is built up. Figures 153-158 show some basic vase shapes as preliminary exercises. The build-up can be made with rings of similar or different diameters. Figures 159-161: vessels with partly smoothed sides. Some rings have been left unsmoothed—this gives good training in proportion. The coarse texture of the surface is achieved by scraping the vessel after drying.

162 B 14

163 A

164 A

Hollow shapes built up from rolls. Plastic ornamentation by sgraffito (Figure 162) and by application (Figures 163, 164). Height of piece on the left: 1 ft. 2 in.

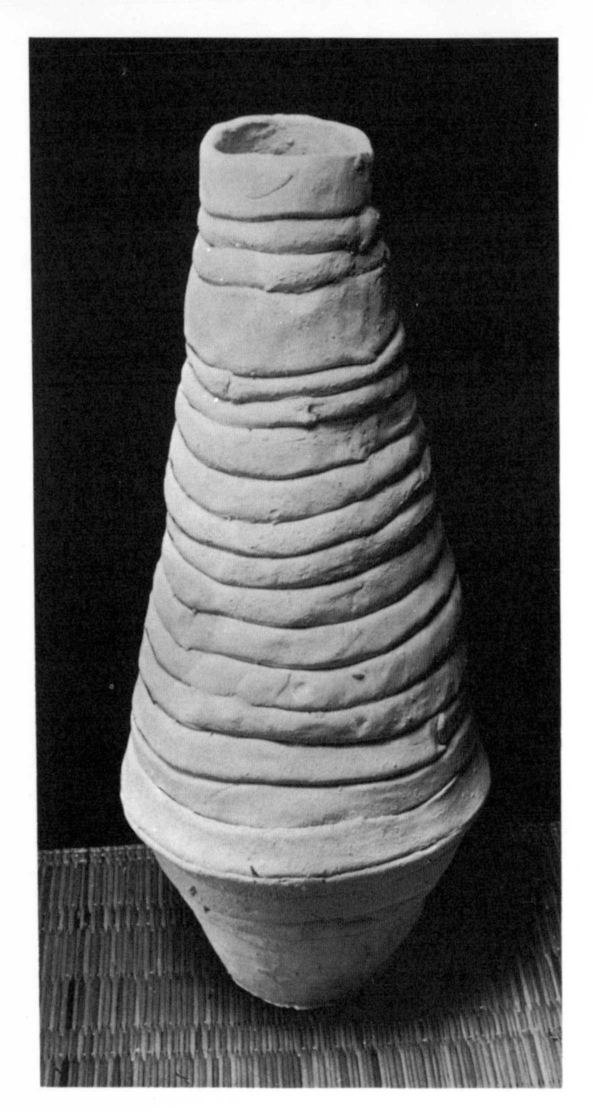

165 S

166 B 14

Figure 165: thin-walled vessel built up from alternate strips and rolls. The rings are not smoothed out.

Figure 166: tall vessel (1 ft. 8 in.). Lively and attractive surface texture, shown by leaving rolls unsmoothed on the outside. A good example of how the working process can produce a decorated surface.

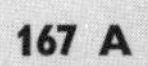

167 A

168 A

169 A

170 B 13, 10, 14

171 B 12, 11, 13

It is essential to ensure that big pieces are produced. Clay is cheap and easy to obtain and there is no need to be restricted to small quantities for reasons of cost, as is the case with plasticine. When setting exercises it is advisable to specify the height and size of piece to be made, to avoid the danger of small, over-neat work. The vessels illustrated here are between four and eighteen inches in height. Some brief remarks on the various types of surface treatment: The rolls and strips have been partially left visible. The left-hand vessel in Figure 167 is built up from loosely rolled and very damp coils, the right-hand vessel has been textured by light finger pressure after smoothing. The rolls of the bowl in Figure 169 have been gently flattened by beating with a ruler. The surface of vessels in Figures 170 and 171 have been sandpapered after drying.

172 B 14

173 B 14

174 S

175 S

176 S

The bottle is perhaps the vessel which is closest to man. Primitive and civilised peoples have used it since time immemorial for the most varied purposes. For thousands of years men have been constantly engaged in shaping it. It is an ideal object for formal artistic training. Perhaps its special attraction is due to its stylised, symbolic representation of the human figure. In these exercises shape, proportion and the relationship between belly, neck and mouth must be very exactly defined.

Bottles, like all tall, narrow vessels, are well suited to being built up from strips.

Figure 174: bottle, resembling a fruit in the organic nature of its shape.

Figure 175: the square base modulates gently into the cylindrical neck.

Figure 176: severe circular shape with vertical sides and neck.

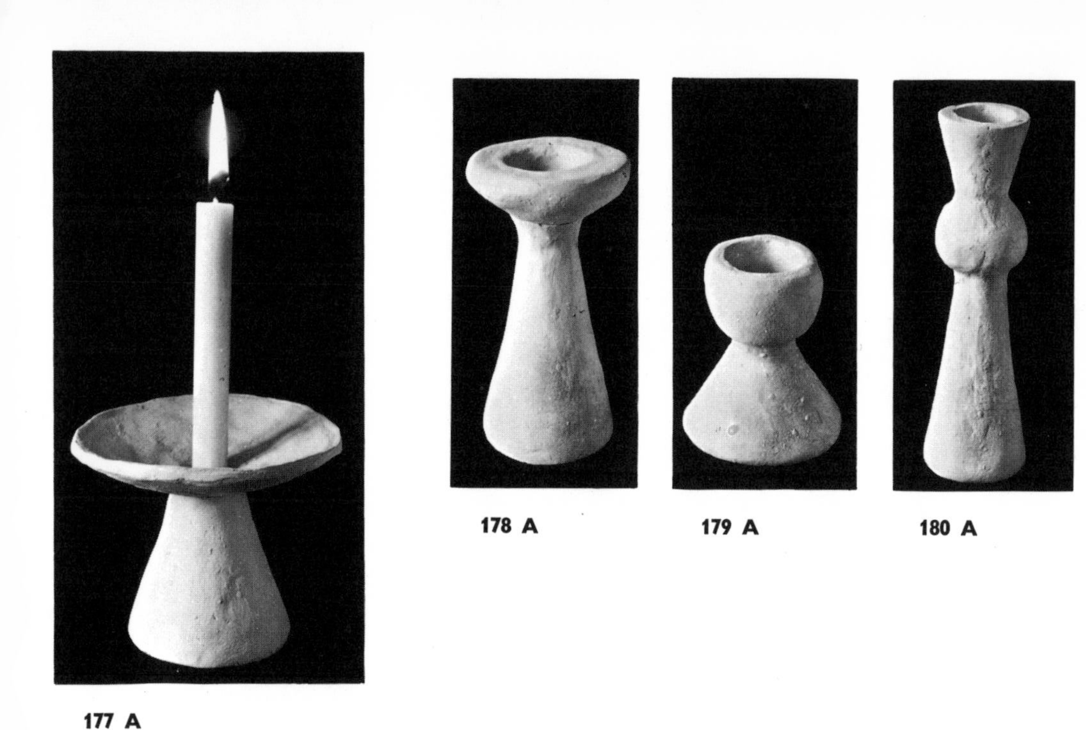

177 A

178 A

179 A

180 A

181 A

The candlestick, like the bottle, is a rewarding subject for modelling practice. Shown here are only a few of the innumerable possible ways of building up candlesticks from cones, or sections of cones and spheres. When putting together the parts care should be taken to make joints as smooth as possible.

182 A

Building up larger vessels requires a certain time. A large pot cannot be made by this method in one session, since the considerable weight of the wet clay would cause it to collapse. The build-up must therefore be done in stages. One section must be dry and strong enough to carry the next before it is added. The upper edge of each section should not be allowed to dry out, but must be kept covered with damp cloths. The body must be well mixed with marl or sand in order to reduce contraction and avoid the vessel cracking as it dries. The scale of a large pot is suited to the coarse texture produced by the mixture of sand or marl with the body.

Height of large pot: 2 ft. 2 in.

Plate III (opposite): various examples of vessels built up from strips, some glazed.

III

183 A

A large plant-pot, diameter 2 ft. 4 in., made by co-operative work. Wide-mouthed pots are particularly difficult to build up as they so easily sag and collapse. Even if built up in stages the sides need to be supported with strips of wood. These larger pieces are best built up in the reverse order, i.e. by beginning with the topmost ring on the tabletop and building up the pot upside down. The base, a round slab of clay, is put on last of all.

184 B 14

185 B 11

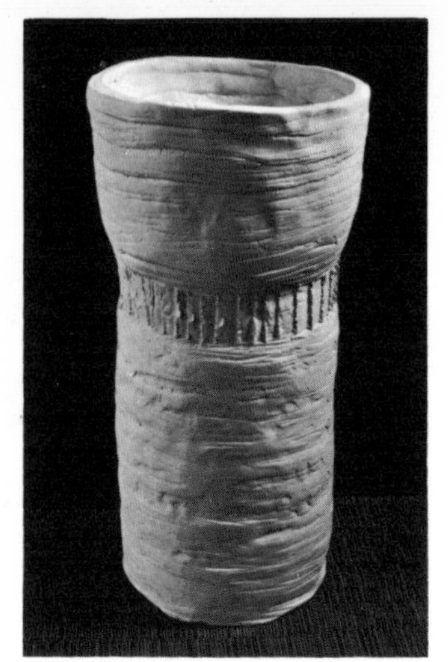

186 S

SURFACE TEXTURING OF HOLLOW PIECES

Shape is the prime element when building up a hollow clay vessel; texture or ornamentation of the surface is secondary—decoration must suit the shape; it should grow from the shape and enhance it. Generally a surface decoration that is integral with the material and brings out its characteristics bears a more valid relation to the shape than any ornament applied as an afterthought. Decoration must always serve shape and above all should never be used to disguise bad workmanship or faulty material. It is most likely to form an organic unity with the shape if it develops as a natural extension of the working process (compare Figures 165 and 166). Methods of surface texturing have already been shown in detail; those used here are finger and stamp methods.

Figures 184-186: examples of stamped decoration—in Figure 184 with a screw-head, in Figure 185 with the point and the blunt end of a pencil and a strip of cardboard. Vessel in Figure 186 flattened with a ruler, the ring impressed with a stamp.

Figure 187: a highly original shape produced by a child, which in spite of an eccentric imagination shows a sure sense of formal values.

189

190

191

192

193 A

194 A

Figures 189-192: boxes, simple and clear in shape, surface decoration by stamping. Surprising effects can be achieved with very simple stamps.

Vessels can also be modelled directly from lumps of clay. This method is valuable for formal exercises and learning the properties of the material, although less suited for practical use.

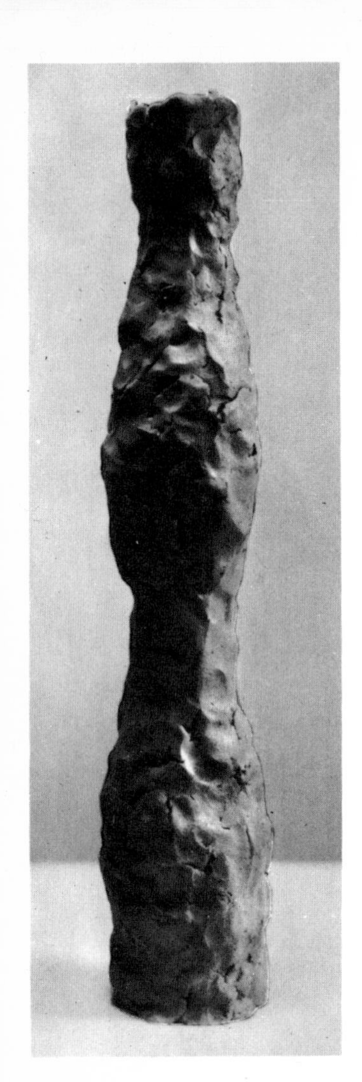

195 G 15

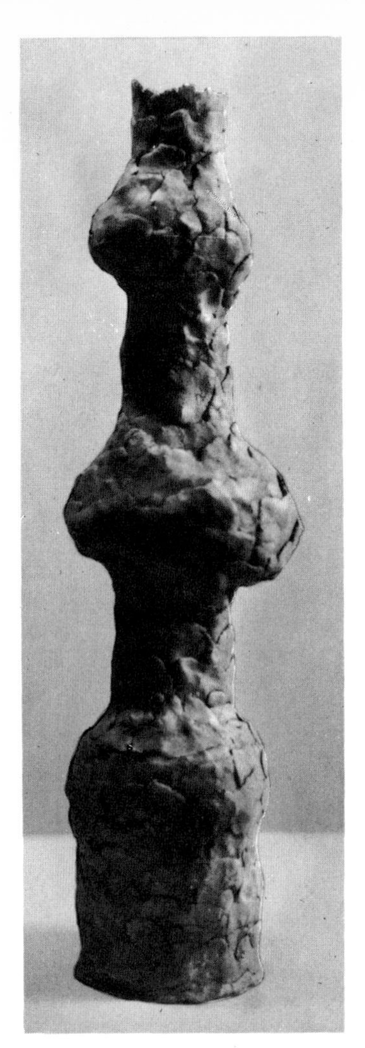

196 G 14

Figures 195, 196: examples of another method of building up hollow pieces. Inspired by the observation of plant forms, thin-walled organic shapes have here been built up out of small flat pieces of clay. Height of vessel on left: 1 ft. 3 in., weight 10 oz.

197 A

198 B 15

FIGURES

Here the same principle of building up is used as in making hollow pots. Making figures by this means depends on maintaining the character of the basic hollow vessel. The technique of build-up by strips forces one to keep to simple shapes and thus to concentrate on essentials. Large, squat forms are therefore well suited as basic shapes for these exercises.

Figure 197: in this piece the working method, i.e. building up by rings, is clearly recognisable. Smoothed on the inside, the ring structure is left visible on the outside.

Figure 198: another treatment of the same exercise. Smoothed inside and out. Dorsal and side fins added afterwards as strips, smoothed into the body and shaped with pressure from thumb and forefinger. The openings (mouth and eyes) are cut out with a knife.

Figures 199, 202: naïve yet strongly expressive forms made by children.

Figure 200: fins and scales added after completing the hollow body.

Page 92 shows examples of how the characteristic shapes of hollow vessels can be happily integrated with natural forms.

In Figures 203, 205 and 206 the shapes were made closed, then cut down the back with a knife and shaped to their final forms. The cock (Figure 206) can be said to represent the ultimate in complexity attainable with this method.

199 **B** 13

200 **A**

201 **A**

202 **B** 13

203 S

204 B 14

205 S

206 S

207 S

Figure 207: the essential character of the bird has been expressed by ruthless simplification. The surface has been textured by scratching with a metal comb in the leather-hard state. Biscuit fired, then partially decorated with coloured glaze. Length of the duck: 18 in.

Figures 208, 209: legs and ears added afterwards to the plain hollow shape built up from strips. The openings were cut out with a knife.

208 B 11

209 B 13

210 S

211 S

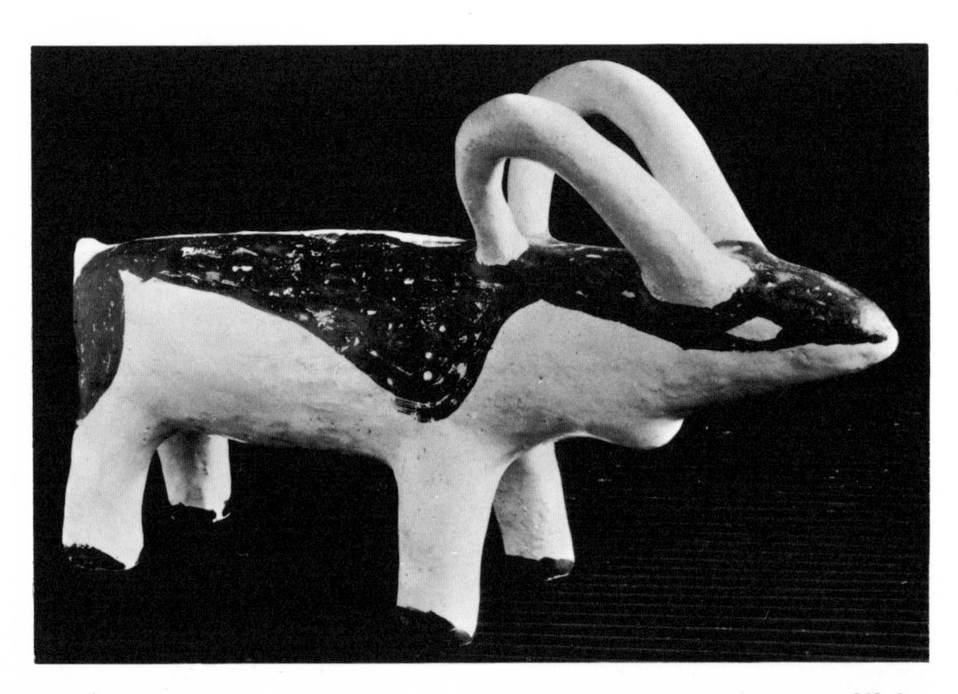

212 S

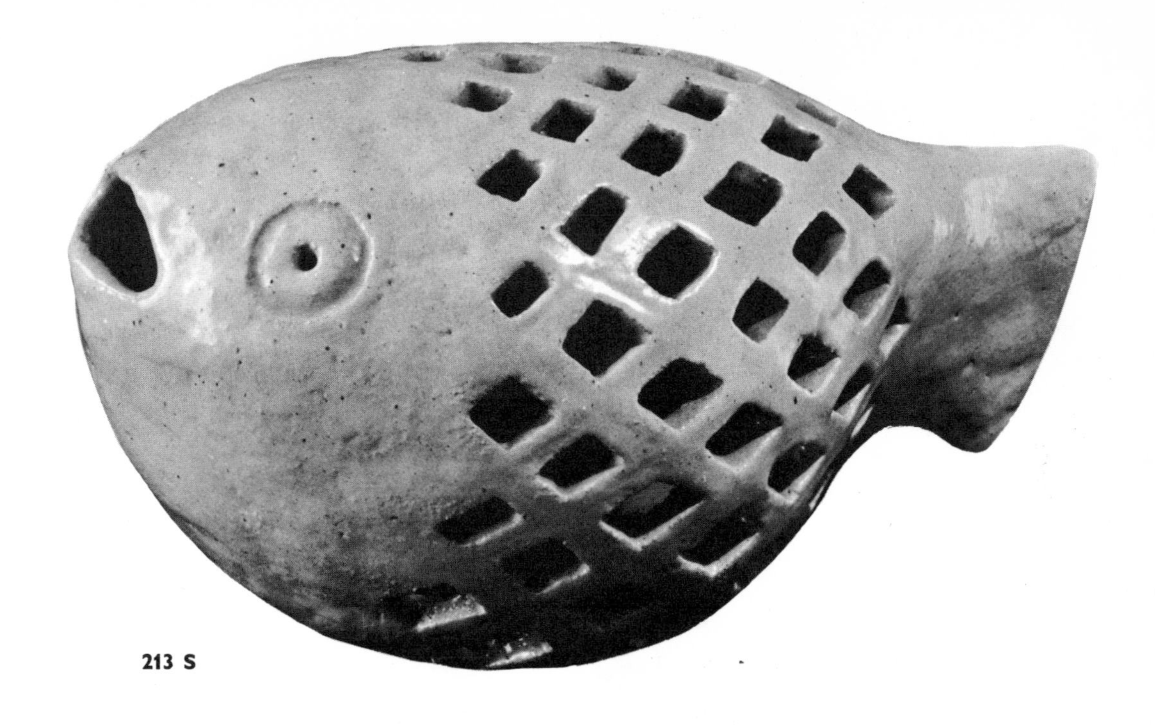

213 S

Figures 210, 211: two results of an exercise to produce figures for a fountain. Characteristic of ceramic forms is the union of horns, legs and tail with the body of the figure.

Figure 212: the large body area is effectively articulated by the use of coloured glaze.

Figure 213: the ceramic characteristics of the form can be emphasised by cutting through the body to show the interior of a hollow piece. Cut with a knife in leather-hard state. Fired, glazed.

214 G 18

Strongly decorative articulation of the simple basic shape with applied spirals and stippling with a pencil-point. Height: 1 ft. 6 in.

Plate IV (facing Page 80): a closed hollow shape was first built up, then cut down the back with a knife to give this result. Biscuit fired.

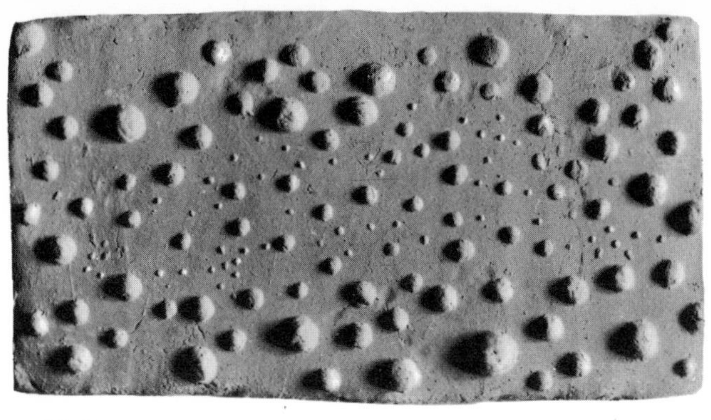

215 S

216 S

Intaglio Cutting

Recesses are cut into a plaster slab with a knife, punch or lino-cutting pen to produce a negative relief or intaglio. When finished the incised slab serves as a die-stamp, similar to a wooden or metal cake mould. To produce an impression, lay a slab of clay on the plaster mould (the clay must be damper than usual, as plaster absorbs water very rapidly) and press the clay carefully into all recesses with the fingers. As plaster will not stick to clay the impression can be easily removed. What was incised in the plaster mould as a negative relief appears as a raised relief on the clay impression. By this method the plastic quality of the relief design is given particular validity. Only by taking an impression from an intaglio can a linear composition be produced with such sharp definition, as the examples on Page 80 show. It is hard for a beginner to visualise the result obtainable from a negative relief. It is therefore advisable to take interim impressions during the work in order to be able to keep a running check on progress.

Figure 215: holes of different depths are cut at random in a plaster slab, which produces this relief texture when a positive impression is taken.

Figure 216: surface texturing produced by circles outlined in relief.

217 S 218 S 219 S

220 S 221 S 222 S

Figure 217: negative plaster mould. Figure 219 shows the impression resulting from it, Figure 218 an impression taken at an interim stage of the work.

Figures 220-222: impressions taken from an intaglio mould at various stages of completion. Each impression can be regarded as a finished piece of work. The vertical linear articulation in the first impression is supplemented in the second by horizontal lines, while in the third certain portions have been cut out to an extra depth in order to appear in the impression as areas of high relief.

Exercises in series such as these are highly instructive. Study of the successive impressions gives a clear indication of how far the incising of the mould is progressing and when to stop.

p. 78 IV

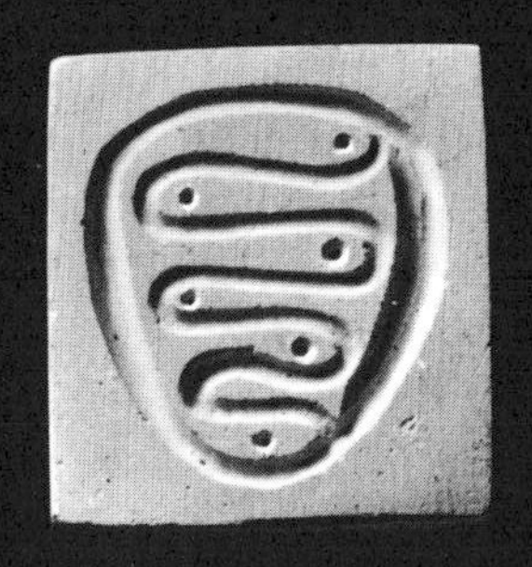

223 S

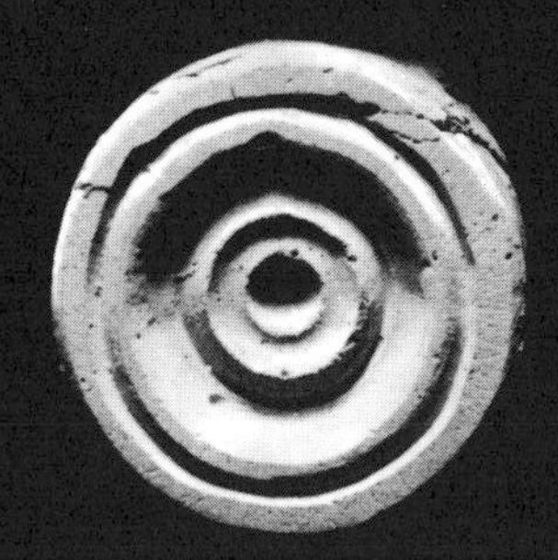

224 S

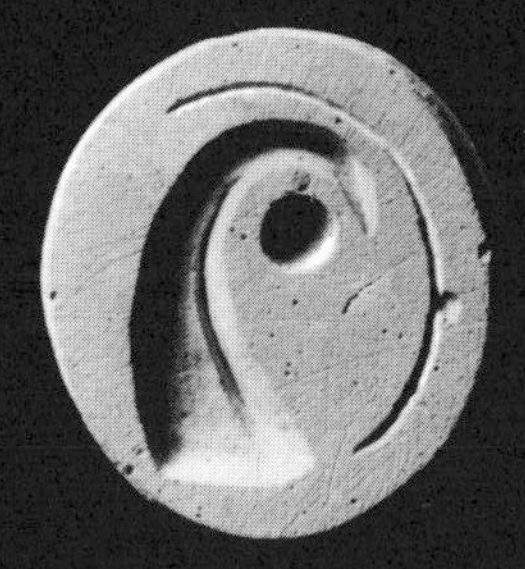

225 S

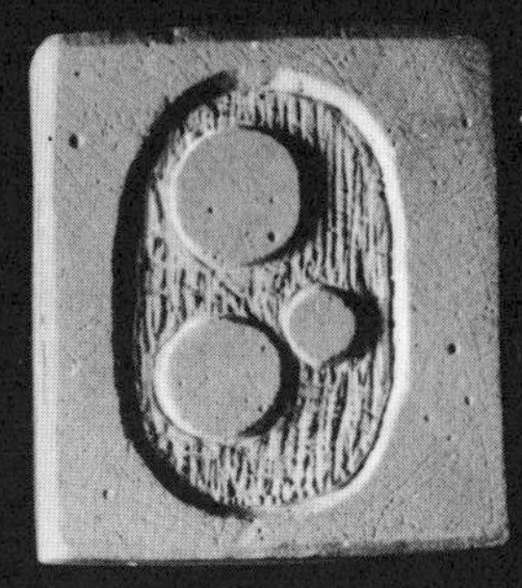

226 S

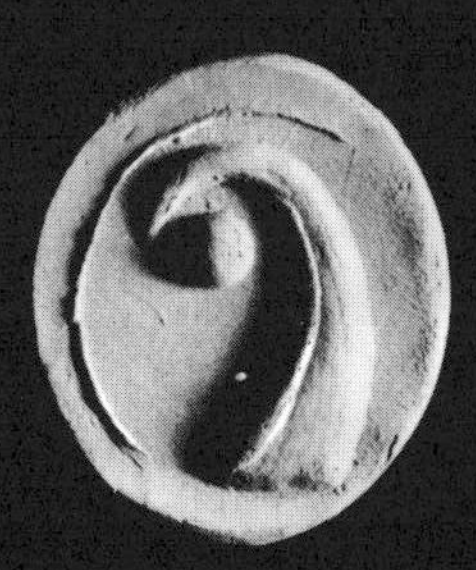

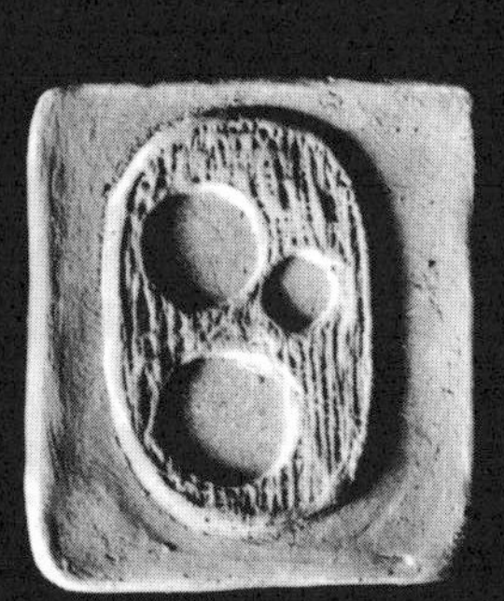

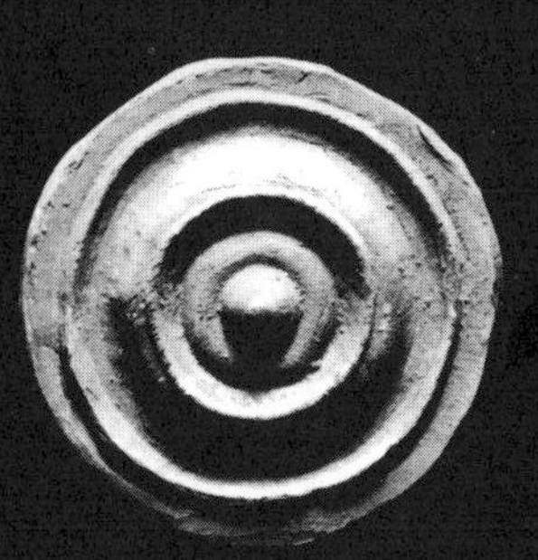

227 S

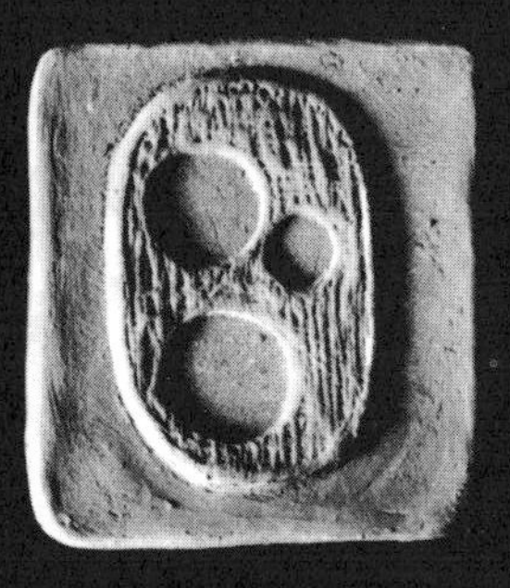

228 S

229 S

230 S

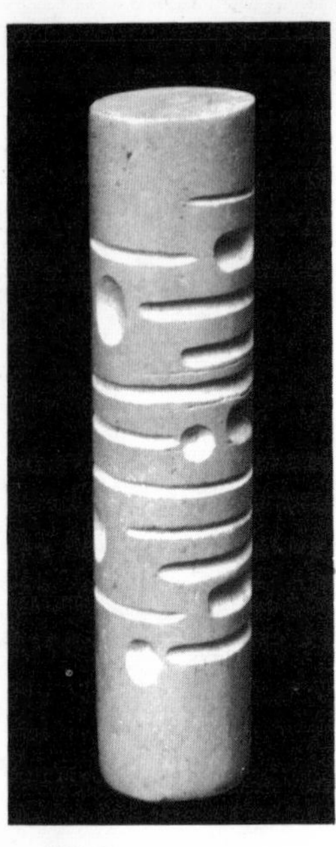

231 S

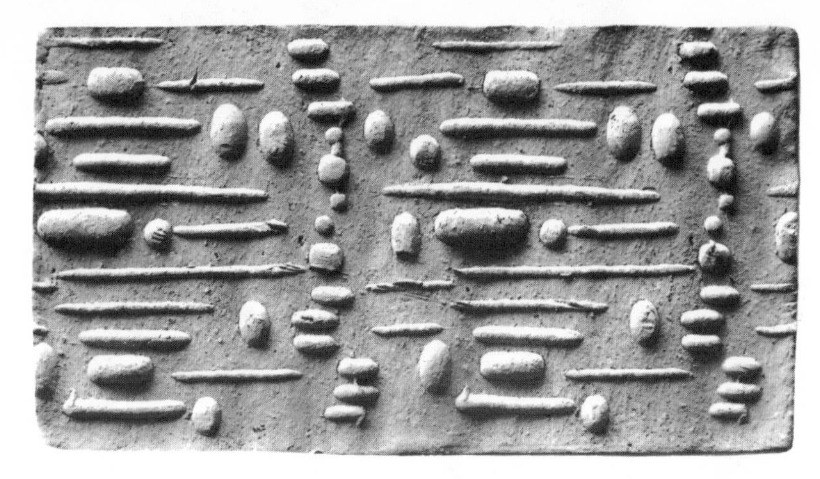

232 S

Since a large number of impressions can be taken from one plaster slab, the process of reverse moulding is very suitable for quantity production. The clay for this use must, of course, be fine-grained. The method is well adapted to making brooches, plaques, pendants, dominoes, draughtsmen etc. This type of work is considerably enhanced if two or more sorts of clay are used which fire to different colours. Natural colours always complement each other, whereas colours that are painted on are at variance with the character of the fired clay. Restraint is also advisable when glazing. A sparing use of glaze is in itself, through the contrast of rough and smooth, matt and shiny, more effective than an all-over glaze.

Figures 223-226 show pattern stamps cut into plaster; Figures 227-230 show the resulting impressions in natural size.

233 S

234 S

Figures 231 and 232 demonstrate a method for producing patterns on a larger scale. A design is cut into a plaster roller; when it is rolled along a damp clay slab the design emerges in relief. The simplest way to make the plaster roller is to cast it in a greased cardboard tube. This method is of great antiquity; the Babylonians and Egyptians used it for impressing seals.

Figures 233, 234: figurative designs produced from reverse-cut moulds.

Tiles patterned in relief have many practical uses, for instance to decorate a wall. They can either be set singly into the wet plaster or arranged in patterns. Whole murals can be built up in this way.

235 **B** 12

236 **B** 9

Free Modelling by Children

In teaching the use of clay, modelling is usually greatly over-emphasised. In this book it has been purposely left until the end and restricted to children's work. Adults' modelling is extremely problematical. In no other form of plastic expression are so many mistakes made. As an amorphous mass clay has no structure. It is easily shaped, can be modelled by adding and taking away and offers no resistance, the possibilities seem infinite. There is a lack of that guidance in the stuff itself that is very marked in other materials, e.g. wood. Even the usual modelling woods impose a certain beneficial discipline on small-scale work. The quality of a plastic shape does not lie in elaboration, but rather in simplification. The ability to create valid plastic forms means being able to summarise a variety of shapes, to subordinate them to the over-all conception and to concentrate on the essential. Children have this ability. They still possess an unconscious feeling for material and form. Children's modelling technique is therefore a good example for adults to follow and this is why only children's work has been selected. The childish pieces illustrated here show in their refreshing directness a striking relationship with primitive ceramics and with the early stages in the development of this art form.

237 B 11

238 B 11

239 B 10

240 G 12

241 B 12

242 G 8

For modelling, enough clay should be provided to allow the use of both hands. Moulds should not be used; by stressing irrelevant detail they are merely distracting. At the most the model can be sparingly textured when finished (Figures 235, 237-239). A pencil is sufficient to bring out the few important details.

Figure 240: modelled with the hands. Details were scratched out of the dried clay with a knife. The hard dried body has a considerable resistance to being worked. This produces simple, severe detailing which is in harmony with the piece as a whole.

Figure 243: any addition of detail to this piece would reduce its effect.

243 B 13

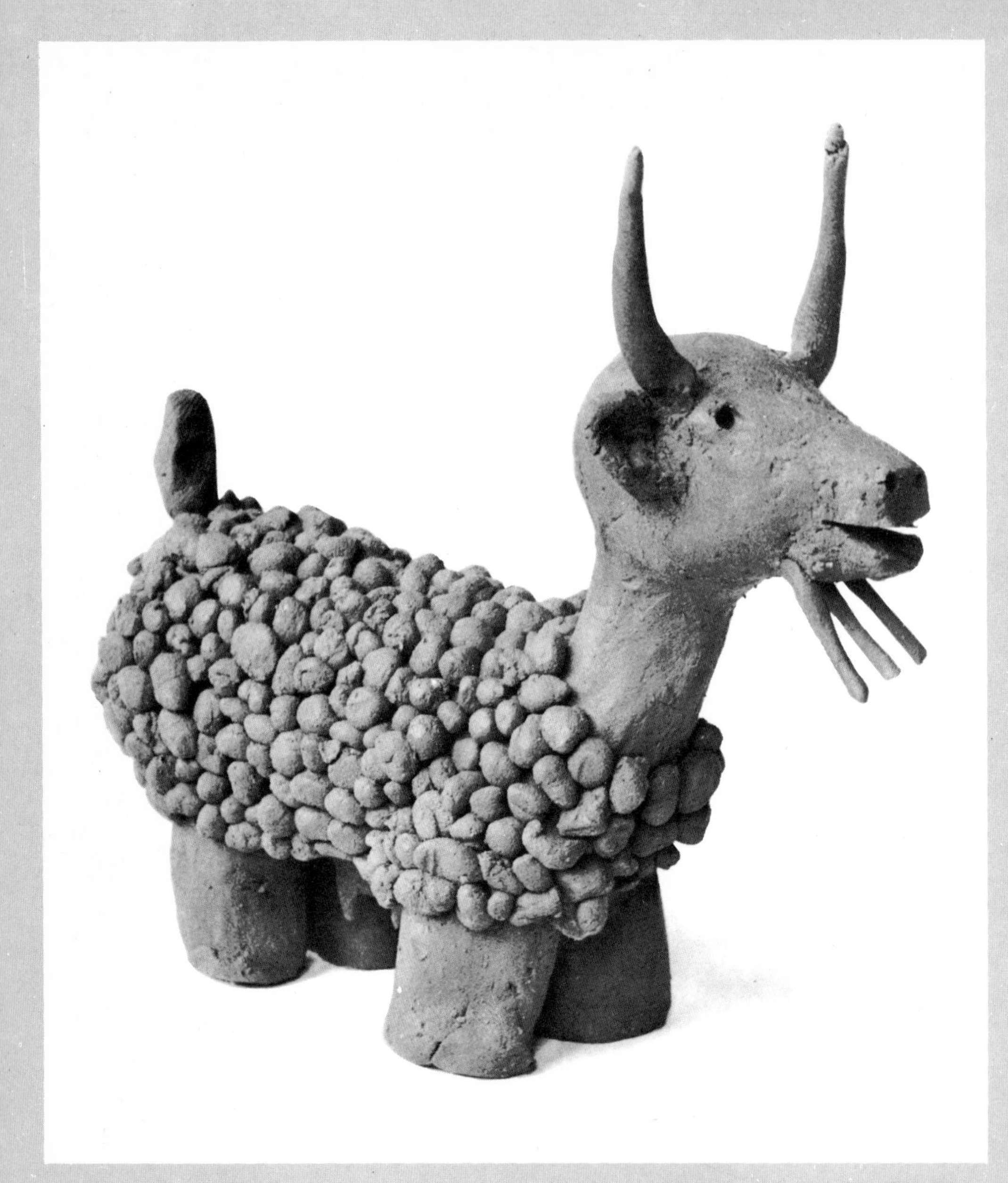

244 B 11

245 B 13

246 B 11

247 B 14

248 B 11

249 B 14

Figure 248: a handsome model by an eleven-year-old. The shaping of the head indicates a sure sense of formal values: although biologically wrong, the placing of the ears is artistically valid.

Figure 249: A lesson in how to model: the essential has been seized and boldly expressed with an absolute minimum of detail.

250 B 12

The purpose of this series of books is not to give technical instruction, but rather to demonstrate methods and to stimulate creative work. Therefore the following notes are limited to essentials.

CLAY

There are innumerable sorts of clay, which vary in colour, grain, composition and in the degrees of plasticity resulting from these factors. The most suitable clays are marl bodies.

Procuring the Clay

1 Clay may be dug straight out of the ground. Generally this is possible only where there are clay-pits nearby. Raw clay must be prepared for use.

2 The easiest, but not always the cheapest, way is to buy professionally prepared ready-to-use clay from a pottery.

3 The cheapest source is a brickworks, where it is best to buy freshly-prepared bricks before they are fired. The body has the correct admixture of sand and when fresh has the right moisture content. The only further preparation required is to knead the body and pick out the stones. Working with brick clay has the advantage that finished pieces can be fired in the brick kiln, as they have the same firing temperature.

4 Finally clay may be bought dry and ready-milled in sacks from potters' merchants. There are prepared bodies for all purposes on the market.

Preparation

Damp clay is split into lumps, thoroughly beaten with a piece of wood or smacked repeatedly on the table and well kneaded with the fingers until a soft, easily workable homogeneous body is produced. Water should be added only with great care and in small quantities. Clay that is too wet smears easily and must often be laboriously dried out again. Dry clay is prepared by dissolving it in water. Powdered clay is mixed with water and stirred in a large vessel to a consistency of thin gruel. Dry lumps, broken and rejected pieces of work are smashed with a hammer before being watered down; when softened they should also be stirred to a gruel. The clay and water 'porridge' should be spread out in as thin a layer as possible to dry on boards, sheets of tin or stone slabs in a well ventilated place. In good weather conditions the clay quickly dries out sufficiently to be kneaded. The best method is to dry the clay on plaster of Paris slabs.

The plaster rapidly absorbs the moisture from the clay, bringing it very quickly to a workable consistency. Plaster slabs can be bought from builders' merchants.

For making hollow pieces, tiles and three dimensional models clay of a particular consistency, so-called modelling clay, is used. Natural clays and prepared throwing clays are too viscous for these purposes. Viscous clays, of very fine grain and recognisable by their greasy sheen are indeed plastic but have a high shrinkage factor (up to 15%) and split easily.

They should be coarsened by mixing with sand or 'grog'. Grog is a kind of clay grit produced by grinding up pieces of fired marl. It can be obtained with a fine (0.5-2 mm. grain size) or coarse grain (2-5 mm. grain size). With very viscous clays it can be added in a proportion of up to 50% of the body. Large hollow pieces require a heavy admixture of grog and are well suited to the surface effect produced by a coarse-grained body.

Storage

Prepared clay is best kept in an earthenware tub or a zinc-lined chest. Zinc or plastic buckets are adequate for small quantities. The containers should be covered with a lid or failing that a damp cloth to prevent the clay from drying out. Plastic bags can be used for keeping very small quantities.

Drying

Finished pieces must be dried slowly, preferably in a heated space where there are no draughts. In drying, clay objects shrink slightly as the body contracts. Large hollow pieces have to be treated with special care. They should be placed on wood (not on stone) and frequently turned round or the moisture will tend to collect in the base. Rims, edges and projecting pieces dry more quickly. To avoid tensions which can lead to splitting, the faster drying of the edges etc. should be retarded by putting damp cloths on them to ensure that the whole piece dries out evenly.

Firing

As soon as a piece has been air-dried, i.e. when the mechanically combined water has evaporated, it can be fired in a ceramics kiln or a brick oven. At firing temperatures of about 600° Centigrade (1112° F.) and upwards (biscuit fire) the chemically combined water is also released, the air-dried clay becomes a firm pottery shard no longer soluble in water. At temperatures of 1100° - 1400° Centigrade (2012° - 2552° F.) the clay vitrifies and the body ceases to be porous.

A hole must be bored in all closed hollow pieces to prevent their cracking open from the air inside them, which expands during the fire.

Surface Treatment before Firing

In a soft state clay can be textured in various ways with stamps, punches or fingers. A smooth surface is obtained by polishing in the leather-hard state. This is done by rubbing the clay smooth with a spatula until it has a dull sheen, or it can be smoothed by patting with a spoon. Leather-hard clay can be scratched or hatched with a metal comb. In the air-dried state the surface can be buffed with sandpaper. Scraping with a knife emphasises the grainy surface texture.

After Firing

Biscuit-fired pieces may be treated with a carborundum wheel or sandpaper. Rubbing with grease or wax is a method of emphasising texture and colour. Biscuit-fired pieces can be made waterproof by dipping in waterglass or a solution of casein. Gloss paint or lacquer should not be used; they destroy the unique character of fired ceramics. Slip dipping and glazing can only be briefly mentioned in these abbreviated technical notes. Glazing in particular (known as glost firing) is an extremely difficult process which demand considerable experience and technical knowledge. Those wishing to learn more are advised to consult specialised handbooks, which contain many essential instructions and recipes.

Slip dipping means covering or patterning one ceramic body with another of a different colour. Slip is a thin, very fine solution of clay in water which fires to the colour of the clay used.

Slip is usually made from a white-firing body, but it can be coloured by the addition of metallic oxides. Slips are also obtainable in ready-mixed powder form. A piece is slip-dipped in the leather-hard state; the slip may also be painted on. After firing, the body is covered with a thin layer of colour. As slip can be scraped after the fire it offers numerous decorative possibilities.

Glaze is the name given to the vitreous coating on ceramic wares. Glazing makes the body waterproof and gives it a hard, shiny surface. As with slip-dipping the piece is covered with liquid glaze mixture after the biscuit fire, or in certain processes in the leather-hard state. As all glazes contain quartz sand, which has a very high melting point, glost firing requires extremely high temperatures.

PLASTER

Various sorts of plaster are to be had from any ironmonger or hardware store (plaster of Paris, stucco, alabastine), and they can be bought in larger quantities from builders' merchants. Plaster of Paris and alabastine harden rather more quickly than stucco. All types are suitable.

To mix, shake the powdered plaster into a bucket or bowl half filled with water (never put water on to plaster) and stir with a stick until it reaches a creamy consistency. The proportions of water to plaster are about 1:1. As plaster hardens in a few minutes the mixture must immediately be poured into the previously prepared moulds. The pail used for mixing must also be washed out at once. For mixing smaller quantities it is best to use a flexible container (a rubber ball cut in half). Solidified remains of plaster can then be broken up and removed by squeezing the container.

Cardboard boxes, tin boxes or wooden cigar boxes can all be used as moulds for casting plaster blocks. It is advisable to support the sides of cardboard boxes with bricks.

Slabs are cast on a base made of glass, plastic or linoleum; the walls of the mould can be a simple wooden frame. All moulds for plaster casting must first be smeared with grease, beeswax or soap to prevent the plaster from sticking to the sides.

The cast can be quite quickly removed from the mould, although thorough drying takes rather longer.

Slabs and blocks can be cut with a tenon saw.

The plaster may be given a texture by the admixture of sand or grog.

Before starting work on plaster it should first be slightly moistened. It will then be easier to cut and the dust is held.

TOOLS

Only a few tools are needed for working clay and plaster. For cutting use a pointed kitchen knife or a penknife. A good instrument for scratching and paring is a book-binder's knife with its short, rigid blade.
Lumps of clay are more easily divided with cutting wire than with a knife. Fasten two short sections of wooden dowel to each end of a piece of thin but strong wire about 2 feet in length; cut a circular groove round the middle of each dowel to prevent the wire from slipping. The best material is rustless brass picture wire. A rolling pin is needed for rolling out clay slabs. Designs are cut in plaster with knife, punch and lino-cutting pen. If there is no suitable tabletop for working, a slightly waxed piece of hardboard is a good substitute. Half-finished pieces can be left on the board when required to put them aside. A broad spatula is useful for cleaning up the working surface. To cut off a slab of clay, hold a well-kneaded block of clay between two wooden laths and slice off a slab of the required thickness with the taut cutting wire, rather as a grocer slices cheese.